GOD'S PROPHETIC BLUEPRINT

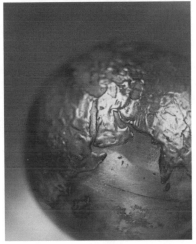

BOB SHELTON

🏛 **BJU PRESS**
Greenville, SC 29614

Library of Congress Cataloging-in-Publication Data

Shelton, Bob, 1929-
  God's prophetic blueprint/Bob Shelton.
    p. cm.
  ISBN 1-57924-397-5 (pbk.)
    1. Bible—Prophecies—End of the world. 2. End of the world—Biblical teaching.
I. Title

  BS649.E63 S54 2000
  263'.9—dc21

                                  00-032253

Note: The fact that materials produced by other publishers may be referred to in this volume does not constitute an endorsement by Bob Jones University Press of the content or theological position of materials produced by such publishers. The position of Bob Jones University Press, and of the University itself, is well known. Any references and ancillary materials are listed as an aid to the reader and in an attempt to maintain the accepted academic standards of the publishing industry.

Photos by PhotoDisc, Inc.

All Scripture is quoted from the Authorized King James Version.

God's Prophetic Blueprint

Edited by Elizabeth B. Berg
Cover and design by Jeff Gray
Illustrations by Emilio D. Rodriguez
Composition by Agnieszka Augustyniak and
Beata Augustyniak

ISBN 1-57924-397-5

15 14 13 12 11 10 9 8 7 6 5 4 3 2 1

DEDICATED

to my beloved wife, Nancy, whose faithful companionship through many years of service for Christ has been my greatest earthly encouragement.

APPRECIATION

I wish to express my sincere thanks to the many dear friends who assisted in the production of this book—with special appreciation to our daughter Becky and her husband, Dr. Mark Kilgus, for their efforts in typing and preparing the manuscript.

CONTENTS

PREFACE

A sizable portion of Scripture deals with the future. In reality it is pre-written history—we call it Bible prophecy. There are prophecies in the Old Testament that were fulfilled in the Old Testament (example—Genesis 15:13). There are prophecies in the Old Testament that were fulfilled in the New Testament (example—Isaiah 7:14). There are prophecies in the New Testament that were fulfilled in the New Testament (example—John 2:18-22). But there are prophecies in the Old and New Testaments that must yet be fulfilled. Jesus had these in mind when He said, "These things must come to pass" (Matthew 24:6).

On the pages that follow it is my desire to write about "these things."

Bob Shelton

Daniel's Seventy Weeks

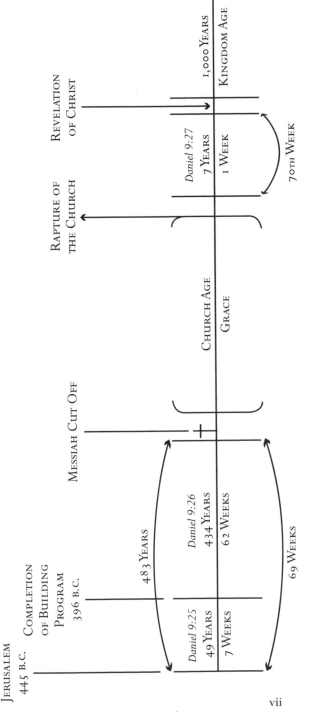

70 Weeks = 490 Years

Daniel's Seventieth Week

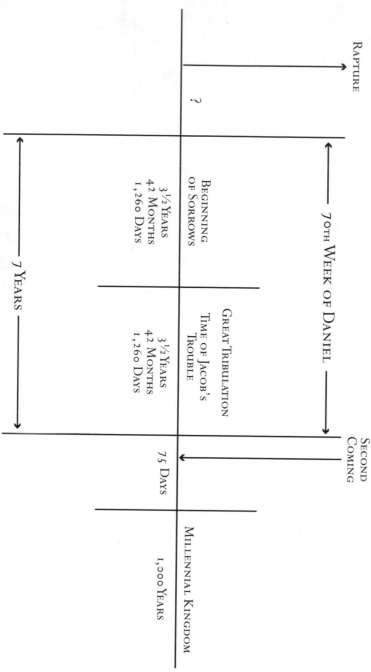

Future Events

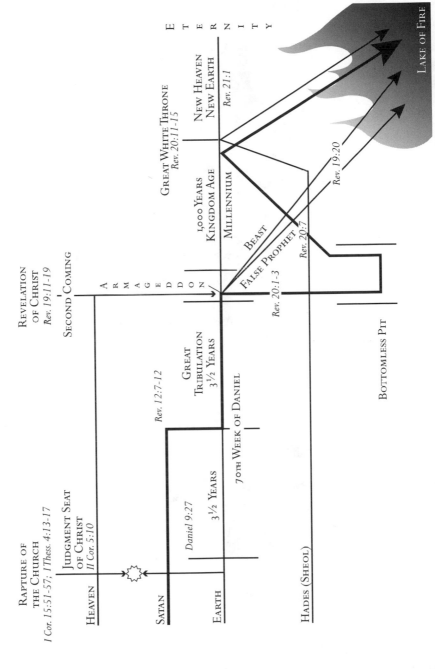

Rapture of
the Church
1 Cor. 15:51-57; 1 Thess. 4:13-17

Judgment Seat
of Christ
II Cor. 5:10

Revelation
of Christ
Rev. 19:11-19

Second Coming

Great White Throne
Rev. 20:11-15

New Heaven
New Earth
Rev. 21:1

ARMAGEDDON

ETERNITY

Heaven

Satan

Earth

Hades (Sheol)

Rev. 12:7-12

Daniel 9:27

3½ Years

Great
Tribulation
3½ Years

70th Week of Daniel

1,000 Years
Kingdom Age

Millennium

Beast

False Prophet

Rev. 20:1-3

Rev. 20:7

Rev. 19:20

Bottomless Pit

Lake of Fire

DANIEL 2:31-43

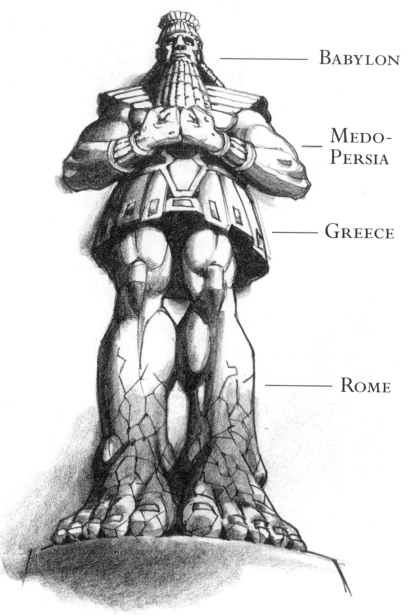

Babylon

Medo-Persia

Greece

Rome

10 TOES - REVIVED ROMAN EMPIRE

Daniel 7:1-8

Greece

Babylon

Medo-Persia

Rome

10 Horns - Revived Roman Empire
Little Horn - The Antichrist

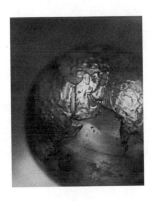

THE RAPTURE OF THE CHURCH

"A MYSTERY"

Paul wrote in his first letter to the church at Corinth:

> Behold, I shew you a mystery; We shall not all sleep, but we shall all be changed, in a moment, in the twinkling of an eye, at the last trump: for the trumpet shall sound, and the dead shall be raised incorruptible, and we shall be changed. For this corruptible must put on incorruption, and this mortal must put on immortality. So when this corruptible shall have put on incorruption, and this mortal shall have put on immortality, then shall be brought to pass the saying that is written, Death is swallowed up in victory. O death, where is thy sting? O grave, where is thy victory? The sting of death is sin; and the strength of sin is the law. But thanks be to God, which giveth us the victory through our Lord Jesus Christ (I Corinthians 15:51-57).

The subject at hand is of vital importance—the Rapture of the church. Please note that Paul begins this passage by saying, "Behold, I shew you a mystery." Many deep and precious truths regarding the catching away of the bride of Christ were still a mystery at this point of God's revelation to man. As puzzling as it may appear, the Old Testament is silent on the subject of the Rapture. A similar void is found in the Synoptic Gospels (Matthew, Mark, and Luke). Even Matthew 24, with its oft-quoted "Then shall two be in the field; the one shall be taken, and the other left" (Matthew 24:40), is not a reference to the coming of Christ for His bride. It is my conviction that the first passage in the Gospels that deals clearly with the Rapture is John 14:2-3. There the Lord Jesus declares, "In my Father's house are many mansions: if it were not so, I would have told you. I go to prepare a place for you. And if I go and prepare a place for you, I will come again, and receive you unto myself; that where I am, there ye may be also." He does not say, "I will come again to the earth," but rather His promise is "I will come again, and receive you unto myself." Though Christ introduces the truth of His coming for His bride in John 14, He does not give us the details of this marvelous event. Consequently, Paul is able to introduce the passage in I Corinthians 15 by saying, "Behold, I shew you a mystery."

"WE SHALL NOT ALL SLEEP"

The Holy Spirit then begins to unravel this mystery as He writes through Paul, "We shall not all sleep." In other words, there will be a generation of believers who will not taste of physical death. This could be that generation. No one on earth knows when Christ will return for His bride. There are many indications that this age is coming to an end, but whether He comes in this generation or not should not deter believers from "looking for that blessed hope, and the glorious appearing of the great God and our Saviour Jesus Christ" (Titus 2:13). The promise is "we shall not all sleep." Paul then goes on to write, "But we shall all be changed."

"WE SHALL ALL BE CHANGED"

I was conducting a series of meetings in a church some years ago and was delighted to see the joy in the heart of the pastor and his people over their newly constructed Christian education building. The pastor was eager for me to see this new facility, so we began to walk down the long corridor. Doors on both sides opened for me to see the various Sunday school departments and classrooms from the oldest age group down to the baby nursery. As we stood before the entrance of the nursery, I saw this appropriate message written above the door: "We shall not all sleep, but we shall all be changed." Obviously, Paul is not speaking in I Corinthians 15 of babies in a nursery but of Christians who are alive at the time of the Rapture. "We shall all be changed." This change is spoken of in other passages of God's Word. For example, Paul wrote, "For our conversation is in heaven; from whence also we look for the Saviour, the Lord Jesus Christ: who shall change our vile body, that it may be fashioned like unto his glorious body, according to the working whereby he is able even to subdue all things unto himself" (Philippians 3:20-21). First John 3:2 reads, "Beloved, now are we the sons of God, and it doth not yet appear what we shall be: but we know that, when he shall appear, we shall be like him; for we shall see him as he is." This truth has brought comfort to countless believers in years gone by and remains a source of encouragement today.

5

In the late 1950s, when my wife and I were missionaries in South Vietnam, I was invited to conduct a Bible conference at a leprosarium high in the beautiful central highlands. I shall never forget the joy of proclaiming God's Word to those precious Christians. In one of the meetings, I felt directed of the Holy Spirit to speak on the subject of the Rapture of the church. In the process of presenting this thrilling truth, we came to I Corinthians 15:52 with its announcement "We shall be changed." At this point, I could not help noticing a dear lady nudge her neighbor with her fingerless hand as if to say, "Did you hear what I just heard? We won't look like this forever!" The fact is that every living child of God will receive his incorruptible body at the Rapture of the church. This will enable believers to pass through any hindrance that might stand in the way as they rise to meet the Lord in the air. In other words, the molecular structure of glorified bodies will not be disturbed as they pass through solid objects. Remember, "we shall be like him." As Jesus passed through the stone walls of the tomb of Joseph of Arimathaea and entered that room "where the disciples were assembled," even "when the doors were shut" (John 20:19), so believers, in their glorified, incorruptible bodies, will be caught up to meet the Lord Jesus Christ in the air without being blocked by any earthly obstacle.

"IN A MOMENT"

Paul goes on to state that the change that occurs at the Rapture will take place "in a moment, in the twinkling of an eye" (I Corinthians 15:52). It has been estimated that the twinkling of an eye is approximately 11/100th of a second. The point is that the Rapture will take place so quickly that no unbeliever on earth will be able to see this great event. Imagine the confusion that will erupt when Christians suddenly disappear. Cars will lose drivers, and planes will lose pilots. There will be people facing each other; suddenly one will be gone. An unsaved person will be talking to his Christian friend by phone when, in an instant, the conversation ends. The question will be asked, "Are you there?" Hundreds of scenarios can be imagined in an effort to present the unbelievable consternation during the moments that follow the Rapture, but the truth to be underscored is that it will happen "in a moment, in the twinkling of an eye."

SOUNDS, NOT SIGNS

Paul continues by announcing that the Rapture will take place "at the last trump" (I Corinthians 15:52). Someone has well said, "We are not looking for signs but listening for sounds." It is true that there are many significant developments in this day that blend into the prophetical picture, but the so-called signs of the times, even those of Matthew 24, are not events that must precede the Rapture of the church. They are signs to those who will be living in Tribulation days that point to the return of Christ in His Revelation (see chart, page ix). The Jews were always looking for signs. "Then said Jesus unto him, Except ye see signs and wonders, ye will not believe" (John 4:48). The day is coming when there will be signs on every hand that will point not only to destruction and judgment for unbelievers but also to that long-awaited day when Christ will return to the earth and set up His kingdom. However, the focus in our text is not "sign" but rather "sound," and there will be at least three of them. Paul mentions one in this text, "the last trump," but he mentions three in I Thessalonians 4:16: "For the Lord himself shall descend from heaven with a shout, with the voice of the archangel, and with the trump of God: and the dead in Christ shall rise first." "A shout," "the voice of the archangel," and "the trump of God" are the three great sounds that will be heard at the Rapture.

The first of these great sounds will be "a shout." "For the Lord himself shall descend from heaven with a shout." This is a military term denoting urgency and authority. One is reminded of our Lord's encounter in John 11 with Lazarus when "he cried with a loud voice, Lazarus, come forth" (John 11:43), and a man who had been dead four days responded to the command of God. When God speaks, things happen! Some day He will call for His bride to leave this earthly scene, and every born-again believer will be caught away.

The second sound will be "the voice of the archangel." It is not surprising that angels will be a part of this picture. They have always been by the side of Christ in His dealings with mortals. They heralded His birth, ministered to Him following His temptation, hovered over His cross, announced His Resurrection, and at His ascension gave a blessed promise to those dazzled disciples. It seems only right that the voice of the archangel should be heard as Christ calls His bride unto Himself.

The third sound will be "the trump of God." As Old Testament prophets used a trumpet to bring the congregation of Israel together, so the day is coming when the heavenly trumpet will sound and Christ will call unto Himself His own ransomed church. The songwriter had this in mind when he penned these words:

> One day the trumpet will sound for His coming,
> One day the skies with His glories will shine;
> Wonderful day, my beloved ones bringing;
> Glorious Saviour, this Jesus is mine![1]

THE DEAD IN CHRIST

Going back to the "mystery" in I Corinthians 15, we see that "the trumpet shall sound, and the dead shall be raised incorruptible." It is essential that we understand where the dead in Christ currently reside before we consider their whereabouts at the time of the Rapture. In II Corinthians 5:8, Paul wrote, "We are confident, I say, and willing rather to be absent from the body, and to be present with the Lord." At the point of physical death, the believer leaves his body and is at once in heaven with Christ. Little wonder that Paul could write, "to die is gain" (Philippians 1:21). One can also appreciate the words of the psalmist: "Precious in the sight of the Lord is the death of his saints" (Psalm 116:15). Death for the child of God is "gain" and a "precious" experience. It is therefore understandable how Paul could write as he did in our text, "O death, where is thy sting? O grave, where is thy victory?" (I Corinthians 15:55).

While pastoring the First Baptist Church of Pontiac, Michigan, I received the sobering news that my predecessor, Dr. H. H. Savage, was dying. Apart from my own father, Dr. Savage had had the greatest influence of any man upon my life. He had been my pastor from my youth. As a matter of fact, he had been my only pastor. I jumped into my car and drove the 180 miles to the hospital in Muskegon because I wanted one more opportunity to talk to him. During my journey, the thought kept returning, "Surely Dr. Savage will give me a nugget today that I will be able to use as the foundation of the message I will preach at his memorial service." I finally reached the hospital, made my way to his room, and slowly walked to his bedside. He looked up and said, "Hello, pastor." I responded, "Hi, pastor." Then with a twinkle in his eye (he had a sense of humor like few men I have ever known), he said, "I've got something very important to tell you." I thought, "Thank You, Lord, here comes my nugget." He went on, "In a few days you'll have my funeral service. The church will be filled with people, and there will be tears and all those things that go along with funerals. But as you look at this body, I want you to remember, it's just the shell—the nut is gone!"

Obviously, I could not quote him a few days later when the service was held, but I got his message in the hospital that day. He was looking death in the face and making a joke of it. He was saying with Paul, "O death, where is thy sting? O grave, where is thy victory?" His was the victory because of the triumph of the Son of God, who paid the penalty of sin by offering His precious blood upon the cross. Paul put it this way: "The sting of death is sin; and the strength of sin is the law. But thanks be to God, which giveth us the victory through our Lord Jesus Christ" (I Corinthians 15:56-57). I incorporated into the message the following poem that Dr. Savage wrote just days before his homegoing:

> This isn't death I'm facing, but it's life forevermore.
> It's not the end I'm nearing; it is ent'ring heaven's door.
> The way ahead is fairer than it's ever been before,
> For it's glory, yes, it's glory over yonder.
>
> There is no fear in thinking I'll soon meet Him face to face,
> The One who proved He loved me by His dying in my place.

> And how I long to thank Him for His mercy and
>   His grace,
> For it's glory, yes, it's glory over yonder.
>
> No pain and no frustrations throughout all the
>   passing years,
> No death nor sorrows present, and no terrors and
>   no fears.
> For He Himself has promised that He'll wipe away
>   all tears,
> For it's glory, yes, it's glory over yonder.
>
> Come quickly, O come quickly, this blest day for
>   which I pine,
> When faith will turn to vision and each promise
>   will be mine,
> And with the hosts of heaven in His presence I will
>   shine,
> For it's glory, yes, it's glory over yonder.

Yes, saints who have died are with the Savior "over yonder."

The Holy Spirit continues to explain the mystery of the Rapture as He inspires His servant Paul to write: "The dead shall be raised incorruptible" (I Corinthians 15:52). The logical question is "If Christians who have died are in heaven with the Savior, then how can they be raised out of their graves?" A perfect cross-reference to the text in I Corinthians is found in I Thessalonians 4. "But I would not have you to be ignorant, brethren, concerning them which are asleep, that ye sorrow not, even as others which have no hope. For if we believe that Jesus died and rose again, even so them also which sleep in Jesus will God bring with him" (I Thessalonians 4:13-14). Believers who have died are with Christ in heaven, and when He returns to rapture His church, He will bring them "with him." If they are to come "with him," then it is obvious that they must originate from the same place. We do not read that He will be coming for them but that they will be coming with Him. Then notice verse 16: "For the Lord himself shall descend from heaven with a shout, with the voice of the archangel, and with the trump of God: and the dead in Christ shall rise first." The logical conclusion is that when Christ returns to rapture His bride, He will stop in the clouds and allow those who are "with him" to return to the places where their bodies were buried. They will then be given their glorified bodies and "shall rise first." Then comes the final act of the Rapture: "We which are alive and remain shall be caught up together with them in the clouds to meet the Lord in the air: and so shall we ever be with the Lord" (I Thessalonians 4:17).

The Rapture is a series of important events:

1. Christ will come from heaven with His saints.
2. He will stop in the clouds.
3. The heavenly host of saints will continue in their descent to the earth to return to the places where their bodies were buried.
4. They will then receive their incorruptible bodies and come out of the graves.

5. We who are alive will also be changed.
6. We shall be caught up together to meet the Lord in the air.

This is the Rapture of the church, and it could occur today. If you know Christ as Savior, I implore you, "Be ye stedfast, unmoveable, always abounding in the work of the Lord, forasmuch as ye know that your labour is not in vain in the Lord" (I Corinthians 15:58). If you have never received God's crucified, resurrected Son as your Savior, I urge you to invite Him to enter your heart while you may.

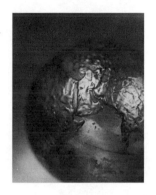

THE TIMES OF THE GENTILES

2

In an in-depth study of Bible prophecy there must be an understanding of two expressions that have their roots in Old Testament Scriptures but will come to fruition in the days ahead. They are "Daniel's seventy weeks" and "the times of the Gentiles." Let us first consider "the times of the Gentiles."

After the reign of King Solomon, internal friction brought a split in the nation of Israel. Solomon's son, Rehoboam, remained king over the Southern Kingdom (Judah) while Jeroboam became king of the ten tribes of the north (Israel). In the following years, there were nineteen kings in the north and twenty kings in the south. The Northern Kingdom lasted from 933 to 721 B.C. It was then that the people were led away by Shalmaneser into Assyrian captivity. The Southern Kingdom lasted from 933 to 605 B.C. It was Nebuchadnezzar who led Judah away into Babylonian captivity. The final deportation and destruction of Jerusalem came in 586 B.C.

NEBUCHADNEZZAR'S DREAM

In the interest of the subject at hand, I would like to return to 605 B.C., which was the beginning of Judah's deportation to Babylon. This date marked the beginning of Gentile rule over the land of Israel and the starting point of "the times of the Gentiles." This important period of human history was later brought into focus through a dream that God gave to

Nebuchadnezzar, a dream the king was unable to remember (see diagram, page x). It is recorded in Daniel 2:

> And in the second year of the reign of Nebuchad-
> nezzar, Nebuchadnezzar dreamed dreams, where-
> with his spirit was troubled, and his sleep brake
> from him. Then the king commanded to call the
> magicians, and the astrologers, and the sorcerers,
> and the Chaldeans, for to shew the king his dreams.
> So they came and stood before the king. And the
> king said unto them, I have dreamed a dream, and
> my spirit was troubled to know the dream. Then
> spake the Chaldeans to the king in Syriack, O king,
> live for ever: tell thy servants the dream, and we
> will shew the interpretation (verses 1-4).

When the magicians, astrologers, sorcerers, and Chaldeans were brought before the king and heard him say, "I have dreamed a dream, and my spirit was troubled to know the dream," they were not the least bit apprehensive. After all, they thought the king simply wanted an interpretation of his dream. Of course, it would be an easy task to conjure up an interpretation. The world is full of modern-day magicians, astrologers, and sorcerers, who are quick to tell us what is going to happen. Beware of these self-appointed "prophets" who make bold declarations of things to come. The true modern-day prophet of God is no more than a humble servant of Christ, rightly dividing the Word of Truth and giving it out under the anointing of the Holy Spirit. God has His ways of separating those who represent Him and those who do not, and it did not take long for King

Nebuchadnezzar to find out who the true servants of the most high God were: "The king answered and said to the Chaldeans, The thing is gone from me: if ye will not make known unto me the dream, with the interpretation thereof, ye shall be cut in pieces, and your houses shall be made a dunghill" (verse 5).

The Chaldeans answered, "There is not a man upon the earth that can shew the king's matter: therefore there is no king, lord, nor ruler, that asked such things at any magician, or astrologer, or Chaldean" (verse 10). At this point,

> Daniel went in, and desired of the king that he would give him time, and that he would shew the king the interpretation. Then Daniel went to his house, and made the thing known to Hananiah, Mishael, and Azariah, his companions: That they would desire mercies of the God of heaven concerning this secret; that Daniel and his fellows should not perish with the rest of the wise men of Babylon. Then was the secret revealed unto Daniel in a night vision. Then Daniel blessed the God of heaven (verses 16-19).

Before considering the dream with its interpretation, please notice that this unusual event was God's way of revealing some very special information regarding the future. Daniel said to the king:

> But there is a God in heaven that revealeth secrets, and maketh known to the king Nebuchadnezzar what shall be in the latter days. Thy dream, and the visions of thy head upon thy bed, are these; As for thee, O king, thy thoughts came into thy mind upon thy bed, what should come to pass hereafter:

and he that revealeth secrets maketh known to thee what shall come to pass (verses 28-29).

This dream, then, had great prophetic significance.

THE RECONSTRUCTED DREAM

The scene changed as Daniel stood before the king and related the forgotten dream:

> Thou, O king, sawest, and behold a great image. This great image, whose brightness was excellent, stood before thee; and the form thereof was terrible. This image's head was of fine gold, his breast and his arms of silver, his belly and his thighs of brass, his legs of iron, his feet part of iron and part of clay. Thou sawest till that a stone was cut out without hands, which smote the image upon his feet that were of iron and clay, and brake them to pieces. Then was the iron, the clay, the brass, the silver, and the gold, broken to pieces together, and became like the chaff of the summer threshing-floors; and the wind carried them away, that no place was found for them: and the stone that smote the image became a great mountain, and filled the whole earth (verses 31-35).

Imagine the reaction of the king as he was once again confronted with his dream. I am not surprised that he later said, "Of a truth it is, that your God is a God of gods, and a Lord of kings, and a revealer of secrets, seeing thou couldest reveal this secret" (verse 47).

THE DREAM EXPLAINED

Daniel gave the interpretation as revealed to him
by God:

> This is the dream; and we will tell the interpreta-
> tion thereof before the king. Thou, O king, art a
> king of kings: for the God of heaven hath given thee
> a kingdom, power, and strength, and glory. And
> wheresoever the children of men dwell, the beasts
> of the field and the fowls of the heaven hath he
> given into thine hand, and hath made thee ruler
> over them all. Thou art this head of gold. And after
> thee shall arise another kingdom inferior to thee,
> and another third kingdom of brass, which shall
> bear rule over all the earth. And the fourth king-
> dom shall be strong as iron: forasmuch as iron
> breaketh in pieces and subdueth all things: and as
> iron that breaketh all these, shall it break in pieces
> and bruise (verses 36-40).

The great image that Nebuchadnezzar saw in his
dream (see diagram, page x) had a golden head
(verse 32). It represented the Babylonian Empire
(verse 38), which came to an end during the reign of
Belshazzar. Daniel 5:31 records the conquest of Dar-
ius the Median. It was he who brought Media and
Persia together, forming the great Medo-Persian
Empire. This empire was pictured in the image as
the breast and arms of silver (Daniel 2:32, 39a).
Many years later, Alexander the Great conquered
Medo-Persia and extended the mighty empire of
Greece. This empire was depicted by the belly and
thighs of brass (verses 32 and 39b). The fourth world
empire was Rome. It remained a united kingdom

until A.D. 364 and then continued on as a divided empire with its western capital in Rome and its eastern capital in Constantinople. Western Rome died in A.D. 476 while the eastern empire continued on until A.D. 1453. There are some who believe the two legs (verse 33) represent eastern and western Rome, but what we know for sure is that the iron legs had their fulfillment in the Roman Empire (verse 40).

So the image that Nebuchadnezzar saw in his dream represented four world empires: Babylon the head of gold; Medo-Persia the silver breast and arms; Greece the brass belly and thighs; and Rome the iron legs. When put together in one fearful image, they present at a glance a period of Bible prophecy called "the times of the Gentiles." It speaks of those times when Israel would be under the control of Gentile power, beginning with the deportation of Judah into Babylonian captivity in 605 B.C.

THE REVIVED ROMAN EMPIRE

All of the empires listed above have made their appearance, but there is one part of the image that is yet to appear. It is associated with the old Roman Empire and is seen in the image as feet (verse 33) with ten toes (verses 41-42). The late H. A. Ironside wrote of this important part of the image:

> This brings us to the last form of the fourth kingdom; for the Roman empire, though at present in abeyance, has not yet come to its end. The ten toes

> on the feet of the image represent ten kings who
> are to reign at one time, but who will form a con-
> federacy on the ground of the ancient empire. This
> is something which the world has never yet seen.[1]

When Dr. Ironside penned these words in 1911, such a merger was the farthest thing from most minds. Today, however, the stage is set for the formation of these ten kingdoms into a confederacy clearly prophesied twenty-six hundred years ago through a dream God gave to Nebuchadnezzar.

Many have tried to tie together the nations that currently exist over the ashes of the old Roman Empire without success. It has been suggested that the children's nursery rhyme "Humpty Dumpty" was originally written about the fall of Rome and the futile efforts of men to reconstruct it. "Humpty Dumpty sat on a wall." He sure did   in the form of the old Roman Empire. "Humpty Dumpty had a great fall." It happened in the year A.D. 476. "All the king's horses and all the king's men couldn't put Humpty together again." There were many who tried—Charlemagne, Napoleon, Bismarck, and Hitler, to name a few.

One indication that the end of this age is near is that for the first time since Rome crumbled, the empire is now emerging again. As we will discover in a later chapter, the ten-nation alliance must come together, for out of it the Antichrist will come. How sobering it is to see that confederacy beginning to form. Though the "ten toes" (revived Roman Empire) may take shape before the church is caught away, the Antichrist cannot appear until after the Rapture. Certainly, the fact that the nations of Western Europe are coming together must be an indication of the lateness of the hour. Many Bible students believe the European Union, previously called the European Common Market or the European Economic Community, is the forerunner of the revived Roman Empire.

In the first printing of this book I wrote,

> It is interesting to note that there are now ten nations in that community. The last to join was Greece, which became a member on January 1, 1981. In 1973, England, Ireland, and Denmark joined. The other six nations are Germany, France, Italy, Belgium, Luxembourg, and the Netherlands.

> One note of caution should be sounded at this point. The fact that there are now ten nations in the European Common Market should not cause one to jump to the conclusion that the final form of the Roman Empire (the ten toes of Daniel 2) is here.

The fact is that there are now fifteen nations in the European Union. Frankly, the Bible does not tell us how many nations will join the European Union. What we know for sure is that from among the nations that occupy the territory of the old Roman Empire, ten will come together in a special alliance. Those ten nations were seen by Nebuchadnezzar in the form of ten toes.

THE END OF THE TIMES OF THE GENTILES

The final part of Nebuchadnezzar's dream is reconstructed by God through His servant Daniel and presented once again to the king:

> Thou sawest till that a stone was cut out without hands, which smote the image upon his feet that were of iron and clay, and brake them to pieces. Then was the iron, the clay, the brass, the silver, and the gold, broken to pieces together, and became like the chaff of the summer threshingfloors; and the wind carried them away, that no place was found for them: and the stone that smote the image became a great mountain, and filled the whole earth (verses 34-35).

"The times of the Gentiles" began when Nebuchadnezzar led God's chosen people into Babylonian captivity twenty-six hundred years ago. Although the Jews began to return to their own country after only seventy years, it really was not their land. They were living on soil that God had given to them, but they were under the control of Gentile powers: Babylon, Medo-Persia, Greece, and Rome.

When God the Son became incarnate in human flesh, His people were living during the days of the fourth Gentile world power, Rome. They longed to be set free to live in their own land under the authority of their long-awaited Messiah. Imagine the excitement in the hearts of those who believed that Jesus was that Messiah and that He would soon break the yoke of Rome and set up His reign of peace.

However, true believers had to be taught that during His first coming to earth, His task was not to bring in the kingdom but to give His life as the only sacrifice for the sin of the world. Some, like Judas Iscariot, would accept Him only as their political leader, who would usher in the Kingdom Age. They were blinded to Old Testament Messianic prophecies, such as Psalm 22 and Isaiah 53, that clearly foretold the death of Christ upon the cross. They, like many today, needed to learn the truth of Christ's Second Coming to earth when He will destroy the total military power of earth in a fearful confrontation called the Battle of Armageddon (see chart, page ix). Then, and only then, will He set up His kingdom here on earth to rule and reign over the affairs of men for one thousand years.

Nebuchadnezzar got a glimpse of Christ's return to earth in the dream God gave to him. Christ is seen as "a stone . . . cut out without hands, which smote the image upon his feet" (Daniel 2:34). As the image came crashing to the ground, "the iron, the clay, the brass, the silver, and the gold . . . became like the chaff of the summer threshingfloors; and the wind carried them away, that no place was found for them" (verse 35). This Old Testament prophecy will surely come to pass, and when it does, "the times of the Gentiles" will come to an end.

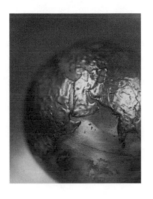

DANIEL'S SEVENTY WEEKS
3

Seventy weeks are determined upon thy people and upon thy holy city, to finish the transgression, and to make an end of sins, and to make reconciliation for iniquity, and to bring in everlasting righteousness, and to seal up the vision and prophecy, and to anoint the most Holy. Know therefore and understand, that from the going forth of the commandment to restore and to build Jerusalem unto the Messiah the Prince shall be seven weeks, and threescore and two weeks: the street shall be built again, and the wall, even in troublous times. And after threescore and two weeks shall Messiah be cut off, but not for himself: and the people of the prince that shall come shall destroy the city and the sanctuary; and the end thereof shall be with a flood, and unto the end of the war desolations are determined. And he shall confirm the covenant with many for one week: and in the midst of the week he shall cause the sacrifice and the oblation to cease, and for the overspreading of abominations he shall make it desolate, even until the consummation, and that determined shall be poured upon the desolate (Daniel 9:24-27).

SEVENTY SEVENS

Verse 24 reads, "Seventy weeks are determined upon thy people." The word *weeks* is an English translation of the Hebrew word *shabua*. It would be better translated "sevens." A clearer rendering of the verse would be "Seventy sevens are determined upon thy people." The Scofield footnote suggests, "These are 'weeks' or, more accurately, sevens of years; seventy weeks of seven years each." God is saying through His servant Daniel that He has determined a period of time for the people of Daniel (the Jews) in which some very special accomplishments will come to pass. The time required will be seventy times seven, or 490 years (see chart, page vii). The first segment of this prophetic timetable would require seven "weeks" (49 years), the second period would be 62 "weeks" (434 years), and the third portion would be one "week" (7 years).

THE FIRST PERIOD

Now, notice the first segment: "Know therefore and understand, that from the going forth of the commandment to restore and to build Jerusalem unto the Messiah the Prince shall be seven weeks, and threescore and two weeks: the street shall be built again, and the wall, even in troublous times" (verse 25). This first part of Daniel's Seventy Weeks would begin when a command would be given "to restore and to build Jerusalem." Remember, Daniel and his people were captives in Babylon. Their hearts yearned to return to their own land. After seventy years, remnants of Jews began returning to Jerusalem for the purpose of restoring the temple. God said it would happen (Jeremiah 29:10).

Then came the year 445 B.C. The temple had been reconstructed, but nothing had been done to restore the walls and the city of Jerusalem. A sober-ing account of the condition of the city was passed along to God's servant Nehemiah: "The remnant that

are left of the captivity there in the province are in
great affliction and reproach: the wall of Jerusalem
also is broken down, and the gates thereof are burned with
fire" (Nehemiah 1:3). Nehemiah responded to this
sad report in the following verse: "And it came to
pass, when I heard these words, that I sat down and
wept, and mourned certain days, and fasted, and
prayed before the God of heaven" (verse 4).

Chapter 2 of the Book of Nehemiah becomes an
indispensable portion of God's Word in a study of
Daniel's Seventy Weeks. Remember, the initiation of
the first segment of seven weeks (forty-nine years)
would be a command "to restore and to build
Jerusalem" (Daniel 9:25). That command is found in
Nehemiah 2:

> And it came to pass in the month Nisan, in the
> twentieth year of Artaxerxes the king, that wine
> was before him: and I took up the wine, and gave it
> unto the king. Now I had not been beforetime sad
> in his presence. Wherefore the king said unto me,
> Why is thy countenance sad, seeing thou art not
> sick? This is nothing else but sorrow of heart. Then
> I was very sore afraid, and said unto the king, Let
> the king live for ever: why should not my counte-
> nance be sad, when the city, the place of my fa-
> thers' sepulchres, lieth waste, and the gates thereof
> are consumed with fire? Then the king said unto
> me, For what dost thou make request? So I prayed
> to the God of heaven. And I said unto the king, If it
> please the king, and if thy servant have found favour
> in thy sight, that thou wouldest send me unto
> Judah, unto the city of my fathers' sepulchres, that I
> may build it. And the king said unto me, (the queen

also sitting by him,) For how long shall thy journey
be? And when wilt thou return? So it pleased the
king to send me; and I set him a time. Moreover I
said unto the king, If it please the king, let letters
be given me to the governors beyond the river, that
they may convey me over till I come into Judah;
And a letter unto Asaph the keeper of the king's
forest, that he may give me timber to make beams
for the gates of the palace which appertained to the
house, and for the wall of the city, and for the
house that I shall enter into. And the king granted
me, according to the good hand of my God upon
me (Nehemiah 2:1-8).

These verses present several important pieces of
information:
- Who gave the command? King Artaxerxes
- To whom was it given?   Nehemiah
- When was it given?   March 14, 445 B.C.

We arrive at the above date because of what is
written in verse 1: "And it came to pass in the
month Nisan, in the twentieth year of Artaxerxes the
king." Artaxerxes ascended the throne of Medo-Persia
in 465 B.C.[1] In his twentieth year as king (445 B.C.),
he gave to Nehemiah the command to return to
Jerusalem and rebuild it. Since no day is given, we
must rely on Jewish custom, which dictates the first
day of the month. The first day of Nisan 445 B.C.
corresponds to our calendar date of March 14 of that
year.

Concerning this intriguing development, Sir
Robert Anderson has written,

> Now the great characteristic of the Jewish sacred
> year has remained unchanged ever since the memo-
> rable night when the equinoctial moon beamed
> down upon the huts of Israel in Egypt, bloodstained
> by the Paschal sacrifice; and there is neither doubt
> nor difficulty in fixing within narrow limits the Ju-
> lian date of the 1st of Nisan in any year whatever. In
> B.C. 445 the new moon by which the passover was
> regulated was on the 13th of March at 7h. 9m. A.M.
> And accordingly the 1st Nisan may be assigned to
> the 14th March.[2]

Returning to Daniel 9:25, we read, "Know therefore and understand, that from the going forth of the
commandment to restore and to build Jerusalem
unto the Messiah the Prince shall be seven weeks."
The command was given on March 14, 445 B.C., and
as God had prophesied through His angel Gabriel,
who in turn passed the vision on to Daniel, the
building program would require seven "weeks"
(forty-nine years). History proved this to be an accurate prediction since exactly forty-nine years were
required to complete the job—the year was 396 B.C.

THE SECOND PERIOD

The second segment of Daniel's Seventy Weeks
was to be a period of 62 "weeks" (434 years). "And
after threescore and two weeks shall Messiah be cut
off" (Daniel 9:26a). That is, 434 years would elapse
from the time the walls and the city were restored
until Messiah would be rejected by His own people
and nailed to a cross. Once again the prediction was

perfect. We are indebted to Sir Robert Anderson for his study of this portion of God's Word. He tells us that Christ made His entrance into Jerusalem on Sunday prior to His Crucifixion. The Julian date was April sixth A.D. 32, which was the tenth of Nisan on the Jewish calandar. (See Exodus 12:1-6.) Anderson then writes:

> What then was the length of the period intervening between the issuing of the decree to rebuild Jerusalem and the public advent of "Messiah the Prince"—between the 14th March, B.C. 445, and the 6th April, A.D. 32? THE INTERVAL CONTAINED EXACTLY AND TO THE VERY DAY 173,880 DAYS, OR SEVEN TIMES SIXTY-NINE PROPHETIC YEARS OF 360 DAYS, the first sixty-nine weeks of Gabriel's prophecy.[3]

Therefore, we conclude, using the Jewish calendar with its 360 days to the year, that there were 69 "weeks" (483 years) from Artaxerxes' command on March 14, 445 B.C., to the day Christ made His entrance into Jerusalem. After that sixty-ninth week came to an end, Messiah was "cut off" (crucified) as God had prophesied.

THE FINAL PERIOD

But there is one "week" (seven years) of time that is yet to be fulfilled. This might well be called "the seventieth week of Daniel." The logical question is "When will it begin?" God tells us through His servant:

> And he shall confirm the covenant with many for
> one week: and in the midst of the week he shall
> cause the sacrifice and the oblation to cease, and for
> the overspreading of abominations he shall make it
> desolate, even until the consummation, and that de-
> termined shall be poured upon the desolate"
> (Daniel 9:27).

The personal pronoun "he" is a clear reference to the "prince that shall come" of verse 26b. Be careful not to confuse "Messiah the Prince" with the "prince that shall come." "Messiah the Prince" is a reference to the Lord Jesus Christ, while the "prince that shall come" speaks of the great impostor, the Antichrist.

According to the prophecy, when this great world leader comes on the scene, he will "confirm the covenant" with the nation of Israel for seven years. At that point, the Jews will believe that this great and powerful leader of the revived Roman Empire is none other than their long-awaited Christ. They will be deceived into thinking they are actually living in the Kingdom Age. In reality, it will be a lull before the storm. In the following chapters, we will take an in-depth look at the counterfeit Christ and the Tribulation to come; but to conclude this chapter, may I remind you that the Seventieth Week of Daniel begins when the Antichrist signs his covenant of peace with the nation of Israel. The Seventieth Week does not begin, as many suppose, at the Rapture of the church (see chart, page viii). There could be several days, even years, between the Rapture and the signing of the covenant. All we know from God's

Word is that the final portion of Daniel's Seventy Weeks, namely the seventieth "week" (seven years), will begin with Antichrist's signing the covenant. That covenant obviously cannot be signed until the Antichrist comes on the scene, and the Antichrist will not surface until the bride of Christ has been caught away. It appears that the coming of Christ for His church must be very near!

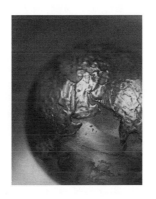

THE COMING OF
ANTICHRIST

There are three questions that should be asked in a study of the person and the work of Antichrist:

- From where will he come?
- When will he arrive?
- What will he do?

In a previous chapter, consideration was given to the fearful image that God presented to King Nebuchadnezzar in a dream twenty-six hundred years ago (see diagram, page x). That image, with its head of gold, breast and arms of silver, belly and thighs of brass, and legs of iron, with "feet part of iron and part of clay" (Daniel 2:33) gives to us at a glance an important piece of the prophetic puzzle called "the times of the Gentiles." Many years later, "Daniel had a dream and visions" from God (Daniel 7:1). Instead of an image of four kinds of metals, Daniel saw four great beasts, but the interpretation was the same (see diagram, page xi). "The first was like a lion, and had eagle's wings" (verse 4). The second beast was "like to a bear" (verse 5). The third was "like a leopard" (verse 6), and the fourth was "dreadful and terrible, and strong exceedingly; and it had great iron teeth . . . and it had ten horns" (verse 7).

As indicated earlier, the vision God gave to Daniel was different from the one He gave to Nebuchadnezzar, but the interpretation is identical. The lion and the golden head represent Babylon. The bear and the silver breast and arms represent Medo-Persia. The leopard and the brass belly and thighs represent Greece. The fourth beast and the iron legs represent

Rome. The ten horns and the ten toes represent Rome revived.

FROM WHERE WILL HE COME?

Then comes an addition. Daniel's dream has something in it that was missing in the dream that God gave to Nebuchadnezzar. Please note Daniel 7:8: "I considered the horns, and, behold, there came up among them another little horn, before whom there were three of the first horns plucked up by the roots: and, behold, in this horn were eyes like the eyes of man, and a mouth speaking great things." Daniel sees in his dream an eleventh horn—a "little horn." It is obvious from the description that this horn represents a man. This man is often spoken about in the chapters and books that follow. He is called by different names, but in each case, he is the same man who is destined to play an important role in the prophetic drama. He is called, among other names, "the prince that shall come" (Daniel 9:26); "the king" (Daniel 11:36); "that man of sin . . . the son of perdition" (II Thessalonians 2:3); "that Wicked" (II Thessalonians 2:8); and "the beast" (Revelation 13:4). The name we know him by best is the "antichrist" (I John 2:22).

Our first question is "From where will he come?" The answer is found in the vision that God gave to Daniel. "I considered the horns, and, behold, there came up among them another little horn" (Daniel 7:8). The Antichrist will arise from among the nations of the revived Roman Empire. We are not told from which of the ten nations he will come, but as surely as God's Word can be trusted, he will make his appearance at just the right moment in the prophetic plan.

WHEN WILL HE ARRIVE?

This brings us to our second question: "When will he arrive?" The key to this important question is found in II Thessalonians 2. Please notice verses 7 and 8: "For the mystery of iniquity doth already work: only he who now letteth will let, until he be taken out of the way. And then shall that Wicked be revealed." The personal pronoun *he* in verse 7 is a reference to the Holy Spirit. At the time of the Rapture, He will "be taken out of the way." This certainly does not mean that He will have no further ministry here on earth after the Rapture. On the contrary, He will be here to convict men of sin and direct them through His Word to Jesus Christ. Certainly, no one could ever be saved apart from the ministry of the Holy Spirit, and multitudes will be saved here on earth following the Rapture. The fact that the Holy Spirit will "be taken out of the way" underscores the truth that the body of a believer is the temple of the Holy Spirit (I Corinthians 3:16); and at the moment believers are caught away when Christ comes for His bride, the Holy Spirit's influence will cease to be felt through the true church. The church will be gone; the light will go out; the salt will be removed. Though the Holy Spirit will be on earth during the Seventieth Week of Daniel, He will step aside temporarily when the church is raptured. Verse 7 then is a reference to the removal of the bride of Christ from this earthly scene. The next verse declares, "Then shall that Wicked be revealed" (verse 8). The coming of Antichrist will follow the Rapture of the church.

WHAT WILL HE DO?

Our final question regarding the Antichrist is "What will he do?" Daniel writes that he will have "a mouth speaking great things" (Daniel 7:8). He "shall do according to his will; and he shall exalt himself, and magnify himself above every god, and shall speak marvellous things against the God of gods" (Daniel 11:36). Paul declares that his "coming is after the working of Satan with all power and signs and lying wonders" (II Thessalonians 2:9). In the Book of Revelation, there is this account:

> Who is like unto the beast? who is able to make war with him? And there was given unto him a mouth speaking great things and blasphemies; and power was given unto him to continue forty and two months. And he opened his mouth in blasphemy against God, to blaspheme his name, and his tabernacle, and them that dwell in heaven (Revelation 13:4b-6).

At last Satan will have his long-awaited counterfeit Christ. The world is looking for such a man at this hour, for we find ourselves at a time in history without great human leadership. As a boy, I can remember the speeches of men like Franklin D. Roosevelt, Winston Churchill, Charles de Gaulle, Adolf Hitler, and Joseph Stalin. These men could sway crowds, influence nations, and turn the tide of history for good or for evil. The basic ingredient common to all of them was leadership.

But where are the leaders today? As far back as 1980 *U.S. News and World Report* quoted historian Ronald Steel:

> I don't see on the horizon the kind of political leadership that can explain to us this new world in which we live. It will take someone with vision to do so, and we have not had that kind of leader for a long time. . . . For now, we are in a time of pygmies when it comes to leadership.[1]

The dearth of great leadership is a significant development as we approach the end of this age; for after the church is raptured, the world will be searching for a man who will be able to lead them. At the right time, from the right place, that man will come.

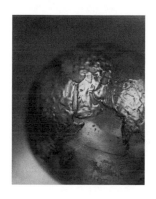

THE SATANIC
TRINITY

5

> And I saw when the Lamb opened one of the seals,
> and I heard, as it were the noise of thunder, one of
> the four beasts saying, Come and see. And I saw,
> and behold a white horse: and he that sat on him
> had a bow; and a crown was given unto him: and he
> went forth conquering, and to conquer (Revelation
> 6:1-2).

The first horseman of the apocalypse is the Antichrist. Notice, he is pictured as riding on a white horse. Be careful not to confuse the rider of the white horse of Revelation 6 with the rider of the white horse of Revelation 19. The latter refers to our Lord Jesus Christ, whose name from eternity past is "The Word of God" (Revelation 19:13).

It is not surprising to discover the subtlety of Satan in seeking to counterfeit the Son of God. In fact, Satan tries to counterfeit everything of God. For example, today there are counterfeit servants of God, counterfeit churches, and counterfeit experiences. Someday Satan will bring about a brief period of peace, which is the best he can do to counterfeit the Kingdom Age; but under Satan's rule, when people are saying, "Peace and safety; then sudden destruction cometh upon them, as travail upon a woman with child; and they shall not escape" (I Thessalonians 5:3).

Perhaps the greatest of all of Satan's counterfeits will be the satanic trinity. It is clearly prophesied in God's Word. Consideration has already been given to the fact that the Antichrist will be the counterfeit of the Lord Jesus Christ. Now, let's look at the counterfeit Holy Spirit: "And I beheld another beast coming up out of the earth" (Revelation 13:11). The first man-beast in this chapter (verses 4-10) is the Antichrist, but in verse 11, another man is also called "a beast." He is the False Prophet. The Antichrist is pictured coming up from among the ten nations of the revived Roman Empire, while it is said that the False Prophet comes "up out of the earth." When we read of "the earth" or "the land" in Scripture without further clarification to pinpoint the location, usually it is safe to assume that the reference is to the land of Israel. In this case, it is clear that the False Prophet will arise from Israel. At this point in Bible prophecy, Satan's masterpiece of the counterfeit trinity is complete:

- Satan will be playing the part of God the Father.
- Antichrist will be the counterfeit Jesus Christ.
- The False Prophet will be the substitute for the Holy Spirit.

It is worth noting that Satan understands the present ministry of the Holy Spirit. No doubt he heard Jesus say,

> When he, the Spirit of truth, is come, he will guide you into all truth: for he shall not speak of himself; but whatsoever he shall hear, that shall he speak: and he will shew you things to come. He shall glorify me: for he shall receive of mine, and shall shew it unto you. All things that the Father hath are mine: therefore said I, that he shall take of mine, and shall shew it unto you (John 16:13-15).

Satan understands that whenever the Holy Spirit is working among men, He glorifies Christ. It seems logical that as soon as the False Prophet makes his appearance, we then read, "And he exerciseth all the power of the first beast before him, and causeth the earth and them which dwell therein to worship the first beast" (Revelation 13:12). It will be the purpose of the counterfeit Holy Spirit to cause every person on earth to worship the counterfeit Christ.

Some years ago while I was preaching in Pennsylvania, the host pastor told me of a friend of his who had become enchanted with turkey hunting. It took quite some time for this modern "Nimrod" to develop his turkey call, but with much persistence, he finally felt prepared to begin his search for the wary prey. After many hours of patient "calling," he heard, off in the distance, the response of a "Tom Turkey." He kept calling, and the turkey kept responding. Finally, the hunter was within a few yards of his prize. As he stood up with his finger on the trigger, much to his astonishment his "turkey" stood up at the same time with his finger on his trigger. You guessed it! Two hunters were gobbling back and forth, and neither was a turkey. They were both counterfeits. I am glad to report that they did not shoot each other, and no doubt they had a good laugh about the situation. But the picture before us in Revelation 13 is no laughing matter because under Satan's direction and empowering, his counterfeits will seek to control the lives of all who live on this planet:

And he causeth all, both small and great, rich and
poor, free and bond, to receive a mark in their right
hand, or in their foreheads: And that no man might
buy or sell, save he that had the mark, or the name
of the beast, or the number of his name. Here is
wisdom. Let him that hath understanding count the
number of the beast: for it is the number of a man;
and his number is Six hundred threescore and six
(Revelation 13:16-18).

Much has been written concerning the mysteri-
ous number of the beast (666), so I will not take
time to rehearse the various interpretations that have
been espoused. What we know for sure is what we
read in this text, namely, that a mark will be im-
posed upon the right hand or forehead of the people
on the earth. Without that mark "no man might buy
or sell" (Revelation 13:17). This will be one way that
Antichrist will seek to eliminate all who refuse to
bow the knee to him, and there will be many. These
dissenters will include the first believers following
the Rapture, the 144,000 Jews from "all the tribes of
the children of Israel" (Revelation 7:4), as well as
millions of other Jewish believers, and multitudes of
Gentiles who trust Christ as Savior (Revelation 7:9).

It appears that Satan is getting the world ready
now for that day when his counterfeit Christ will
impose his "mark" in an effort to control the people
by monitoring all business transactions. A cashless
society appears imminent with the growing use of
ATMs and debit cards. Using computers for online
banking and paying bills over the Internet is also

gaining in popularity. "Cellular phones and other mobile wireless devices may soon supplement home computers for handling transactions."[1] For those people who are concerned about the security of such systems, new technology is being used that identifies an ATM customer using scans of the iris of his eye.[2] Man now has the capability of putting invisible, but permanent, numbers on our bodies in the form of laser tattoos. Such numbers show up under infrared scanners at checkout counters. Due to the tremendous gains in electronics technology, computers have the capacity of handling fund transfers for all of the people on earth. For example, one such giant computer is now resting in Luxembourg, one of the fifteen nations of the European Union and perhaps one of the ten nations represented by the toes of the image of Daniel 2. Surely the stage is being set for the coming of Antichrist, who will, according to the prophetic plan, seek to control the buying and selling by all the people on earth.

The satanic trinity will appear to have their way in all of the affairs of men, but as we shall see, the true God who has been on His throne from eternity past will be triumphant in His battle with the forces of Satan.

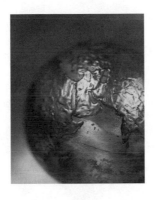

THE NORTHERN
CONFEDERACY MEETS
THE WRATH OF GOD

> And the word of the Lord came unto me, saying,
> Son of man, set thy face against Gog, the land of
> Magog, the chief prince of Meshech and Tubal, and
> prophesy against him, And say, Thus saith the Lord
> God; Behold, I am against thee, O Gog, the chief
> prince of Meshech and Tubal: And I will turn thee
> back, and put hooks into thy jaws, and I will bring
> thee forth, and all thine army (Ezekiel 38:1-4*a*).

In Ezekiel 39:2, God declares that He will bring a mighty army to "the mountains of Israel" and will also "turn [them] back." With God's hooks in its jaws, this army will invade the land of Israel and will experience its greatest military defeat. As we consider this portion of God's prophetic plan, I would like to ask four questions:

- Who leads the invasion?
- Why is there an attack?
- When will it occur?
- What is the result?

WHO LEADS THE INVASION?

First, who leads the invasion of Ezekiel 38? Most students of Bible prophecy are convinced that verse 2 is a reference to the land of Russia: "Son of man, set thy face against Gog, the land of Magog, the chief prince of Meshech and Tubal, and prophesy against him." In Genesis 10:1, the generations of Noah are listed. Noah had three sons, Shem, Ham, and Japheth. Notice that among the sons of Japheth are mentioned "Magog . . . Tubal, and Meshech" (Genesis 10:2). Scofield is accurate in stating, "From

Magog are descended the ancient Scythians, or Tartars, whose descendants predominate in the modern Russia." Meshech and Tubal were also progenitors of those peoples who moved northward and, in turn, became the fathers of those who later established what we know today as Russia. It is believed that the city of Moscow derived its name from Meshech, and Tobolsk received its name from Tubal.

The Russian Bear will not be alone in its effort to devour the little nation of Israel; its allies are presented in Ezekiel 38:5-6: "Persia, Ethiopia, and Libya with them; all of them with shield and helmet: Gomer, and all his bands; the house of Togarmah of the north quarters, and all his bands: and many people with thee." It is interesting to note that the first nation mentioned that will unite its forces with Russia in this attempt to destroy Israel is Persia. The name Persia was changed in 1932 to Iran. Dwight Pentecost writes,

> Allied with Russia will be Iran (Persia), certain
> Arab states (Put or Ethiopia), Germany, and some
> Asiatic peoples known as Togarmah, which may in-
> clude an extensive coalition of Asiatic powers. That
> this is not an exhaustive list is seen from Ezekiel
> 38:6: "and many people with thee."[1]

The leader of this mighty northern confederacy will be Russia.

In 1979 Richard Nixon's secretary of state Henry Kissinger wrote a book about his White House

years. Kissinger recalled a 1972 conversation with
Soviet ambassador Anatoli Dobrynin in which

> he [Dobrynin] lost his cool only once when I asked
> him how the Soviet Union would react if the
> 15,000 Soviet soldiers in Egypt were in imminent
> danger of being captured by Israelis. Dobrynin be-
> came uncharacteristically vehement and revealed
> more than he could have intended: "First of all, we
> never put forces somewhere who can't defend
> themselves. Second, if the Israelis threaten us, we
> will wipe them out within two days. I can assure
> you plans are made for this eventuality."[2]

Although Russia's military power today is not
what it was during the height of the Cold War, "for
the first time since August 1991, some Russian leaders are openly saying the military-industrial complex
should be restored to its former status."[3]

WHY IS THERE AN ATTACK?

The second question is "Why such an attack?"
Part of the answer is a common hatred for the Jews.
There have always been men on the scene like
Haman, who would have slain all of the Jews in
Medo-Persia if God had not intervened. Twenty-five
hundred years after Haman's time a mad ruler by the
name of Hitler decided to kill as many Jews as possible within his empire. Not long after the conflict between Iran and Iraq began, Iran sent a communiqué
to Iraq that encouraged a united war against Israel
instead of fighting each other. But more than hatred
for Jews enters into the picture before us. May I

suggest that hunger for material gain will also excite Russia and its allies.

In Ezekiel 38:12, it is written that this great army will come "to take a spoil." Israel is known as the "gateway to three continents." It has been called "the navel of the earth." The Dead Sea is known as "the jewel box of the Orient." There is no way of computing the total wealth of that sea with its vast mineral resources. But beyond the actual worth of Israel is the fact that the day may come when the oil of the Middle East will be available only to those nations that position themselves against Israel. As far back as 1979 Yasser Arafat, leader of the Palestine Liberation Organization, responded to a question put to him: "Is Arab oil committed to the Palestine cause?" His answer: "Definitely, and do not forget . . . the socialist countries will be in need of oil."[4]

In a *Reader's Digest* article dated June 1980, an editor introduces the article with these words: "Encouraged by American indecisiveness, the Russian Bear is once again on the prowl. Unless we take a strong stand now, says this expert, control of the vital Middle East oil spigot could end up in Soviet hands."[5] The day will come, according to God's Word, when Russia will move against Israel "to take a spoil" (Ezekiel 38:12).

WHEN WILL IT OCCUR?

Our third questions is "When will Russia come against Israel?" Obviously, the invasion of Ezekiel 38 could not take place until a nation called "Israel" existed. It is clear from the context that Russia not only will be interested in a piece of Middle Eastern real estate called Israel but also will be even more desirous of destroying a nation of people. The prophecy is clear:

> Therefore, son of man, prophesy and say unto Gog, Thus saith the Lord God; In that day when my people of Israel dwelleth safely, shalt thou not know it? And thou shalt come from thy place out of the north parts, thou, and many people with thee, all of them riding upon horses, a great company, and a mighty army: And thou shalt come up against my people of Israel (Ezekiel 38:14-16a).

In the past, liberal theologians have scoffed at this prophecy by citing that Russia would have great difficulty destroying a nation that did not exist. It is true that since 605 B.C. the Jews had been unable to claim the land of Israel as their own (except briefly during the days of the Maccabean revolt). They were always under the heel of foreign Gentile empires. Even when Jesus was there, the land was under Roman control.

For twenty-six hundred years, the Jews had not been in their own land, or if they were, it did not belong to them. In other words, since Nebuchadnezzar led Judah away into Babylonian captivity at the beginning of "the times of the Gentiles," the Jews had not been able to claim the land that God gave them as their own. Then came God's prophetical announcement that a great northern confederacy would some day come "against the mountains of Israel" (Ezekiel 38:8) to destroy or conquer the "people of Israel" (Ezekiel 38:16). The question of liberal theologians was "How could Russia come against a nation that did not exist?" Imagine the confusion in liberal circles when in 1948 the United Nations created a home for Jews in the land of Palestine. On May 14 of that year, British control came to an end; and for the first time in twenty-six hundred years, the Jews were in their own land ruling their own affairs.

Of course, God said it would happen. Consider for a moment the following passage from Ezekiel 37:11-12:

> Then he said unto me, Son of man, these bones are the whole house of Israel: behold, they say, Our bones are dried, and our hope is lost: we are cut off for our parts. Therefore prophesy and say unto them, Thus saith the Lord God; Behold, O my people, I will open your graves, and cause you to come up out of your graves, and bring you into the land of Israel.

One of the most significant prophetical developments of our day has been the return of the Jews from all over the world to the land of Israel. They have returned from no fewer than 120 nations, speaking at least 83 different languages. I grant you they are returning, for the most part, in unbelief. That is, they are not aware of the truths of Ezekiel

37 and 38, nor are they willing to receive the Lord
Jesus Christ as their Messiah; but the day will come
when the scales will fall from their eyes. They will
see that God caused them to come together (Ezekiel
37:7) as the dry bones in Ezekiel's vision came together. They will recognize God's power in opening
their "graves" (a reference to the Gentile nations of
earth) and bringing them "into the land of Israel"
(Ezekiel 37:12). The prophecy will be fulfilled that
declares,

> And ye shall know that I am the Lord, when I have
> opened your graves, O my people, and brought you
> up out of your graves, And shall put my spirit in
> you, and ye shall live, and I shall place you in your
> own land: then shall ye know that I the Lord have
> spoken it, and performed it, saith the Lord (Ezekiel
> 37:13-14).

Our question is "When will the invasion occur?"
Obviously, it could not occur until after Israel became a nation. That has now taken place and Israel
is, at last, independent and self-governing. It should
also be noted that the invasion out of the north cannot take place until Israel is "at rest." "And thou shalt
say, I will go up to the land of unwalled villages; I
will go to them that are at rest, that dwell safely, all
of them dwelling without walls, and having neither
bars nor gates" (Ezekiel 38:11). I must take exception with those who believe the invasion of Ezekiel
38 is imminent. There are those who believe the
next major prophetic event will be the destruction

of the armies of Russia against the mountains of Israel. They believe this must happen before Antichrist will be revealed in the world. In reality, the only prophetic event that is imminent is the coming of Christ for His bride. This event (the Rapture of the church) could take place before you finish reading this chapter. But there are several events that must precede the invasion of Israel by the northern confederacy. In proper sequence, they are

1. The Rapture of the church
2. The coming of Antichrist
3. The signing of his covenant with Israel (Daniel 9:27)
4. The Jews' belief that their long-awaited Christ is ruling over them, that they are actually living in kingdom days
5. The establishment of Israel as "the land of unwalled villages . . . at rest, that dwell safely" (Ezekiel 38:11)

It is obvious that Israel is not dwelling safely today. It is not the land of "unwalled villages." On the contrary, about one-third of Israel's national budget goes for defense. The invasion of Israel cannot take place today because Israel is not at peace. Israel is not at peace because the covenant of Daniel 9:27 has not been signed. The covenant has not been signed because Antichrist has not yet been revealed, and Antichrist has not been revealed because the church has not been raptured. Certainly, the coming of Christ for His bride is near.

WHAT IS THE RESULT?

Our final question is "What will be the results of the invasion?" In Ezekiel 38:18-19, we read: "And it shall come to pass at the same time when Gog shall come against the land of Israel, saith the Lord God, that my fury shall come up in my face. For in my jealousy and in the fire of my wrath have I spoken, Surely in that day there shall be a great shaking in the land of Israel." God will begin His judgment on the northern armies by sending an earthquake. Notice "a great shaking." This will, no doubt, create such panic within the ranks that "every man's sword shall be against his brother" (Ezekiel 38:21b). To add to the confusion and destruction, we read "And I will plead against him with pestilence and with blood; and I will rain upon him, and upon his bands, and upon the many people that are with him, an overflowing rain, and great hailstones, fire, and brimstone" (Ezekiel 38:22). It is interesting to compare God's judgment upon Egypt prior to the Exodus with His judgment in Ezekiel 38. "So there was hail, and fire mingled with the hail" (Exodus 9:24). When fire and ice come out of heaven at the same time, you can be sure God is at work! Ezekiel 38 concludes with these words: "Thus will I magnify myself, and sanctify myself, and I will be known in the eyes of many nations, and they shall know that I am the Lord" (Ezekiel 38:23).

A Soviet report of space exploration broadcast on Radio Moscow and monitored in the U.S. announced, "We have not discovered God. We have turned out lights that no man will be able to turn on again. We are breaking the yoke of the Gospel, the opium of the masses. Let us go forth, and Christ shall be relegated to mythology."[6] In essence, this report said that Russia's probes into space have not produced evidence that there is a God. The fact is, nobody finds God by probing into space. Man cannot reach God by rockets. We find Him revealed through His blessed Word, the Bible, and those who seek for Him there with a "whole heart" will surely find Him (Psalm 119:2, 10; Deuteronomy 4:29).

The great Northern Bear has admitted he has looked for God and cannot find Him. The day is coming when he will not be looking, but God will manifest Himself. The destruction will be hard to fathom. The account in Ezekiel 38 and 39 is not the Battle of Armageddon. We will come to that part of the prophetic plan in a chapter that follows.

WHEN BLIND EYES SEE

The Seventieth Week of Daniel will begin when Antichrist confirms a covenant with the nation of Israel (Daniel 9:27). This promise of peace, from the one the Jews believe to be their long-awaited Messiah (actually the Antichrist), will cause the Jews to relax. The covenant will allow them to carry on their Old Testament order of worship, including animal sacrifices. They will be certain that the Kingdom Age has begun.

It will become obvious, however, that they have been tricked by "the man of sin" because soon after they let down their guard and become "the land of unwalled villages . . . at rest, that dwell safely" (Ezekiel 38:11), the northern confederacy, led by Russia, will "ascend . . . like a storm" (verse 9) in an attempt to destroy the nation of Israel. It will become clear to truth-seeking Jews that the rider of the white horse of Revelation 6 is the Antichrist (verse 2). The next rider comes on a red horse "to take peace from the earth" (Revelation 6:4). Jews will reason, "How could the first rider be our Christ when the second rider brings war, for when the true Messiah comes, He will bring peace?"

It should also be noted that during those days, 144,000 "servants of . . . God" will be proclaiming the truth of the gospel of Jesus Christ (Revelation 7:3). In addition, the faithful ministry of the "two witnesses" will be felt (Revelation 11:3). Scales will fall from Jewish eyes as they admit that their real Messiah came "unto his own, and his own received him not" (John 1:11). They will remember how they cried for His blood and finally found satisfaction when He was nailed to a cross. Isaiah 53 will be understood:

> He is despised and rejected of men; a man of sorrows, and acquainted with grief: and we hid as it were our faces from him; he was despised, and we esteemed him not. Surely he hath borne our griefs, and carried our sorrows: yet we did esteem him stricken, smitten of God, and afflicted. But he was wounded for our transgressions, he was bruised for our iniquities: the chastisement of our peace was upon him; and with his stripes we are healed. All we like sheep have gone astray; we have turned every one to his own way; and the Lord hath laid on him the iniquity of us all (verses 3-6).

At last they will understand God's timetable. The first coming of Messiah was to give His blood on the cross as the only atonement for the sin of the world (Psalm 22). The second coming of Messiah (the Revelation of Christ—see chart, page ix) will be to set up His kingdom here on earth (Psalm 24).

God's Word does not reveal how many Jews will turn to Christ as Savior, but one word of clarification should be made. When we read in Romans 11:26 that "all Israel shall be saved," we are not to understand that every Jew will come to Christ. It is true that Israel as a nation is to be saved, but not every Jew will respond to the truth of the gospel. As we shall discover in a later chapter, when Christ returns to the earth in His Revelation, He will find not only believing Jews (called "wise" virgins in Matthew 25) but also unbelieving Jews (called "foolish" virgins). We know that the virgins without oil in their lamps (Matthew 25:3) are unbelievers because Christ will say to them, "I know you not" (Matthew 25:12). Though many Jews will refuse to receive Christ as Savior, there will, no doubt, be millions who will be saved.

In addition to Jewish Tribulation saints, there will be millions of Gentiles who will open their hearts by faith to the Lord Jesus (Revelation 7:9). It is safe to say that more people will turn to Christ during the Seventieth Week of Daniel than during any comparable period of time in all of human history. It should also be noted that a great percentage of Tribulation saints will be "beheaded for the witness of Jesus, and for the word of God, and which had not worshipped the beast, neither his image," nor would they receive "his mark upon their foreheads, or in their hands" (Revelation 20:4). There will be a great turning to Christ as penitent sinners, Jews and Gentiles alike, open their hearts to the crucified, resurrected, and soon-coming Son of God.

THE GREAT
TRIBULATION

8

Daniel 9:27 is the key to understanding the starting point of the Seventieth Week. It will begin when "the prince that shall come" (Antichrist) "confirm[s] the covenant" with the nation of Israel (Daniel 9:26b, 27). Verse 27 also holds the key to the beginning of the Great Tribulation: "And in the midst of the week he shall cause the sacrifice and the oblation to cease." Remember, the Seventieth Week of Daniel is a period of seven years; so when we read "in the midst of the week," we are to understand at the halfway point, after three and one-half years, the Great Tribulation will begin. When Antichrist causes "the sacrifice and the oblation to cease," he breaks a promise he made to the nation of Israel three and one-half years earlier.

The fact that animal sacrifices will no longer be permitted will be enough to persuade many Jews that they have been deceived. They will see that their "great leader" is not their long-awaited Messiah but the prophesied "man of sin," the Antichrist. Other developments will also serve to open the eyes of blinded Jews. For example, Antichrist will cause "all, both small and great, rich and poor, free and bond, to receive a mark in their right hand, or in their foreheads" (Revelation 13:16). The true Messiah would never allow such a thing, for God would never command people to do something He had clearly forbidden. In Leviticus 19:28, God declared: "Ye shall not . . . print any marks upon you: I am the Lord."

Perhaps the greatest indication that the Roman prince is the counterfeit Christ is found in Daniel 9:27: "And in the midst of the week he shall cause the sacrifice and the oblation to cease, and for the overspreading of abominations he shall make it desolate." This passage must be associated with Matthew 24:15: "When ye therefore shall see the abomination of desolation, spoken of by Daniel the prophet, stand in the holy place, (whoso readeth, let him understand)." The "abomination of desolation" is a reference to Antichrist, who will enter the temple, "stand in the holy place," and declare to the world that he is God. The apostle Paul adds these words regarding the uplifting of Antichrist: "[He] exalteth himself above all that is called God, or that is worshipped; so that he as God sitteth in the temple of God, shewing himself that he is God" (II Thessalonians 2:4).

Then will come what some have called "the ultimate sacrilege." Antichrist will have an image made of himself. The image will appear to be human, for it will be able to speak, and those who will not worship the image must be found and killed (Revelation 13:14-15). It appears that the image will actually be located in the holy of holies of the temple, for it is written, "And from the time that the daily sacrifice shall be taken away, and the abomination that maketh desolate set up, there shall be a thousand two hundred and ninety days" (Daniel 12:11).

Once again truth-seeking Jews will see the real identity of Antichrist. They will reason, "He cannot be our Messiah, for the true Christ would never give a command that would conflict with His own law." And the law is clear:

> Thou shalt not make unto thee any graven image,
> or any likeness of any thing that is in heaven above,
> or that is in the earth beneath, or that is in the
> water under the earth: thou shalt not bow down
> thyself to them, nor serve them: for I the Lord thy
> God am a jealous God (Exodus 20:4-5a).

The days that follow will be the most horrible days of suffering and death this planet has ever experienced. They are the days of the Great Tribulation (see chart, page ix). The apostle John saw those days in the revelation God gave to him on the isle of Patmos (actually, the "Revelation of Jesus Christ," Revelation 1:1). Beginning with chapter 6, we are introduced to the seal judgments, which include the four horsemen of the apocalypse.

The remaining seal judgments, as well as the trumpet and vial judgments, bring death to so many millions that the majority of people alive at the beginning of the Great Tribulation will be dead within the 42 months (or 1,260 days) that follow. For example, let us look at just two of the judgments that John sees:

> And I looked, and behold a pale horse: and his
> name that sat on him was Death, and Hell followed
> with him. And Power was given unto them over the
> fourth part of the earth, to kill with sword, and
> with hunger, and with death, and with the beasts of
> the earth (Revelation 6:8).

From this single judgment, one-fourth of all the people on earth will die. Their deaths will come from war, hunger, and ravenous animals. In Revelation 9:16 we read of a mighty army of two hundred million soldiers that will move from the Far East to the land of Israel. As they make their journey, they will "slay the third part of men" (Revelation 9:15).

If there were only those two judgments (fourth seal and sixth trumpet), we could conclude that 50 percent of all the people on earth will die. But we cannot stop the death count with just two judgments. There are seven seal judgments; seven trumpet judgments; and seven vial, or bowl, judgments. Though we have no way of knowing for sure how many people will perish, it seems from the slaughter of the northern confederacy (Ezekiel 38) through the Battle of Armageddon (Revelation 19) that at least two-thirds of all the inhabitants of earth will die. My heart aches to think that some who read these words may reject the Lord Jesus Christ as Savior and be a part of the scene we have considered in this chapter. I plead with you, come to Christ now, while you may.

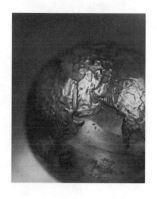

THE BATTLE OF
ARMAGEDDON

9

And it was given unto him to make war with the
saints, and to overcome them: and power was given
him over all kindreds, and tongues, and nations.
And all that dwell upon the earth shall worship
him, whose names are not written in the book of
life of the Lamb slain from the foundation of the
world. If any man have an ear, let him hear (Revelation 13:7-9).

From this portion of God's prophetic blueprint, it
appears that Antichrist will have everything going his
way. He will have power "over all kindreds, and
tongues, and nations," and he will be the undisputed
ruler of the planet. In addition to his exalted position, he will be worshiped by all who "dwell upon
the earth," with the exception of those who have
trusted God's crucified Lamb as Savior (Revelation
13:7-8).

For nearly three and one-half years, the satanic
trinity will appear to have absolute control over the
affairs of men. In Daniel's prophecy we read, "And
the king shall do according to his will; and he shall
exalt himself, and magnify himself above every god,
and shall speak marvellous things against the God of
gods, and shall prosper till the indignation be accomplished" (Daniel 11:36). But then a strange turn of
events will take place: "And at the time of the end
shall the king of the south push at him" (Daniel
11:40a).

It is important to understand that directions in
Scripture, unless otherwise designated, are usually

related to Israel. That is, when we read of "the king
of the south," it is to be understood that the text is
speaking of that kingdom south of Israel. Most students of Bible prophecy are convinced that this is a
reference to Egypt. The day is coming when "the
king of the south" (Egypt) will "push at him," the Antichrist. Here is a revolt in the making. It appears
from the following verses that the rebellion will be
subdued, at least temporarily. Then comes bad news
for the Antichrist from other quarters of his world
kingdom: "But tidings out of the east and out of the
north shall trouble him" (Daniel 11:44). Here is a
full-scale revolt. The Russian Bear will have had at
least three and one-half years to lick the wounds
from his humiliating defeat by God (Ezekiel 38), and
he is now ready to join forces with the kings of the
east in an uprising against the forces of Antichrist.
The prophecy of Daniel 11 is a revolt against the
Roman prince. On the one side will be the revived
Roman Empire (the first ten nations to come under
the control of Antichrist) plus the rest of Western
Europe and those countries that were born of European influence. These nations will all remain loyal to
Antichrist. On the other side will be the revolting
nations of Daniel 11, including the king of the south
(Egypt), the king of the north (Russia), and the kings
of the east.

Once again directions must be related to Israel.
The kings of the east are those kings east of Israel.

They can be identified further from Revelation 16:12: "And the sixth angel poured out his vial upon the great river Euphrates; and the water thereof was dried up, that the way of the kings of the east might be prepared." It is clear to see that the kings of the east are east of Israel and also east of the river Euphrates. They are the kings of the Far East. We read further of these kings and their movements toward Israel in Revelation 9:

> And the sixth angel sounded, and I heard a voice from the four horns of the golden altar which is before God, saying to the sixth angel which had the trumpet, Loose the four angels which are bound in the great river Euphrates, And the four angels were loosed, which were prepared for an hour, and a day, and a month, and a year, for to slay the third part of men. And the number of the army of the horsemen were two hundred thousand thousand: and I heard the number of them (verses 13-16).

Imagine, as this mighty army of two hundred million moves from the Far East to unite forces with the kings of the north and south for the great showdown with the armies of Antichrist, it will destroy "the third part of men." That is, as the army from the Far East makes its way to the land of Israel for the great battle, it will kill one out of every three people on earth. One wonders how any system could be so ruthless. Certainly, we are seeing the warm-up in our day for such a massacre.

My wife and I served the Lord as missionaries in the Far East for ten years. Our children were all born in the Orient. Becky and Shari were born during our first term on Okinawa, and Dan was born during our second term in Saigon. We had planned to spend our lives in South Vietnam, but the advance of Communism changed those plans. Of course, God was not caught by surprise. I mention this phase of my ministry for Christ to add a bit of credibility to that which appears in this book on the subject of Communism. I know what it is to hide from Viet Cong soldiers in the Mekong Delta. I have felt the pain of losing fellow missionaries, six of whom were killed in a single attack on their mission compound in the tribal city of Benme Thuot. Three other missionary friends were captured in the leprosarium nearby and were never heard from again. Other missionaries were martyred for Christ, and hundreds of national believers were ruthlessly murdered, some of them skinned alive. I know what it is to have Vietnamese pastors write to cancel planned crusades because Communist soldiers had threatened their lives if they permitted me to preach in their churches.

In the years that followed our return from South Vietnam, my heart ached to hear of the indescribable atrocities that took place in that troubled little nation. Our smaller neighbor to the west was hit even harder by the rising tide of Communism. It has been reported that at least two and one-half million of

Cambodia's seven million were murdered within a period of three years.

I was in Hong Kong in 1952 when tens of thousands of Chinese were fleeing from the mainland. Their hope was to make it to the British crown colony of Hong Kong. Some of them tried to swim, while others came on small boats and homemade rafts. Many of the swimmers did not make it in those shark-infested waters. Hundreds of boats and rafts were carried out into the ocean by sudden storms and disappeared. Some of those people who successfully arrived in Hong Kong shared with me stories of indescribable cruelty on mainland China. I was told of great holes that were carved out of the ground by bulldozers. Then hundreds of villagers were forced to stand beside those open graves as Communist machine guns opened fire. The bulldozers then came back to finish their gruesome work.

These stories, as horrible as they are, cannot compare to the mass slaughter that is coming, according to Bible prophecy. The armies of the kings of the east will someday move in a westward direction to unite forces with other nations in an attempt to destroy the armies of Antichrist. As the kings of the east make their move, they will "slay the third part of men" (Revelation 9:15). The logical question is "Why will the nations of earth be divided into two factions at this point in Bible prophecy?" John Walvoord in his fine book *Armageddon* gives us the

answer as clearly as any that I have read on this subject:

> Why will Satan organize a world war to disrupt his
> world kingdom? Satan's desperate strategy will be
> much more important than his control of the world
> through the world dictator. Although from their
> point of view they are gathered to fight it out for
> world power, the armies of the world will actually
> be assembled by Satan in anticipation of the second
> coming of Christ. The entire armed might of the
> world will be assembled in the Middle East, ready
> to contend with the power of Christ as He returns
> from heaven. As subsequent events make clear, the
> movement will be completely futile and hopeless.
> The armies of the world are by no means equipped
> to fight the armies of heaven. Still, Satan will as-
> semble the nations for this final hour and, in fact,
> the nations will choose to side with Satan and op-
> pose the second coming of Christ. It will be the
> best that Satan can do. These events will give the
> nations their choice and allow Satan his desperate
> bid to oppress Christ's second coming.[1]

After all, Satan cannot announce to the world that
Christ is about to return to the earth in His Revelation, for he has convinced his followers that the tri-
une God is himself, his christ, and his prophet.

As the Seventieth Week of Daniel nears its conclusion, Satan must have a way of gathering the entire military power of earth to Israel, for Satan
knows God's prophetic plan. He knows that Christ
promised to return to the earth following the Great
Tribulation. I am sure that he has read the account of

Christ's ascension in Acts 1 with the promise of His
return:

> And when he had spoken these things, while they
> beheld, he was taken up; and a cloud received him
> out of their sight. And while they looked stedfastly
> toward heaven as he went up, behold, two men
> stood by them in white apparel; which also said, Ye
> men of Galilee, why stand ye gazing up into
> heaven? this same Jesus, which is taken up from you
> into heaven, shall so come in like manner as ye have
> seen him go into heaven. Then returned they unto
> Jerusalem from the mount called Olivet, which is
> from Jerusalem a sabbath day's journey (verses 9-
> 12).

Satan is also aware of the promise in Zechariah
that "his [Christ's] feet shall stand in that day upon
the mount of Olives" (Zechariah 14:4*a*). As the Seventieth Week nears its end, Satan will devise his
master strategy, namely, to put the spirit of revolt
into the hearts of the king of the south, the king of
the north, and the kings of the east. His plan will be
to divide the armies of earth into two divisions, and
then to bring the total military power of this planet
to Israel for what they think will be a great world
war. In reality, it will be Satan's way of gathering the
nations of earth in an attempt to defy the eternal
God.

It is clear from God's prophetic Word that Satan
will use demonic power to bring the armies of earth
to Israel.

And I saw three unclean spirits like frogs come out of the mouth of the dragon, and out of the mouth of the beast, and out of the mouth of the false prophet. For they are the spirits of devils, working miracles, which go forth unto the kings of the earth and of the whole world, to gather them to the battle of that great day of God Almighty. Behold, I come as a thief. Blessed is he that watcheth, and keepeth his garments, lest he walk naked, and they see his shame. And he gathered them together into a place called in the Hebrew tongue Armageddon (Revelation 16:13-16).

Now we come to that great confrontation when the "stone . . . cut out without hands" will smite the "image upon his feet" (Daniel 2:34). Consider these sobering words from Revelation 19:

And I saw heaven opened, and behold a white horse; and he that sat upon him was called Faithful and True, and in righteousness he doth judge and make war. His eyes were as a flame of fire, and on his head were many crowns; and he had a name written, that no man knew, but he himself. And he was clothed with a vesture dipped in blood: and his name is called The Word of God (verses 11-13).

Who is this one on the white horse? His name is called "The Word of God." In John 1 we read: "In the beginning was the Word, and the Word was with God, and the Word was God" (John 1:1). Here is the record of the one who was with God and at the same time was God, whose name was the Word of God. This eternal person then became a man, for verse 14 declares, "And the Word was made flesh, and dwelt among us, (and we beheld his glory, the glory as of the only begotten of the Father,) full of grace and truth." It is clear from this passage that Bethlehem was not the beginning of God the Son. When He took a body, He also took the name "the Lord Jesus Christ"; but from eternity past, His name was "The Word of God." This will be the name He bears as He descends from heaven in His Revelation.

"And the armies which were in heaven followed him upon white horses, clothed in fine linen, white and clean" (Revelation 19:14). Here is a reference to those who know Christ as Savior, for at the Rapture of the church (at least seven years prior to the return of Christ to the earth) believers will receive their glorified bodies and their garments of white. Together they will enjoy the fellowship of Christ and one another in heaven while the earth is going through its horrible time of tribulation. Finally, they will gather around their heavenly Bridegroom and enjoy the "marriage supper of the Lamb" (Revelation 19:7-9). Then they will follow Christ as He descends from heaven to do battle with the total military power of earth. Please note that they are called "the armies which were in heaven" (Revelation 19:14). It is true that believers will be in that heavenly army, but it will not be necessary to fight, for the record reads, "And out of his mouth goeth a sharp sword, that with it he should smite the nations: and he shall rule them with a rod of iron: and he treadeth the winepress of the fierceness and wrath of Almighty God" (Revelation 19:15).

The weapon that God will use in His confrontation with the forces of Satan will be the most powerful weapon of all time, His Word. Imagine the thoughts that will be racing through the minds of "the beast, and the kings of the earth, and their armies" as they are "gathered together to make war against him that sat on the horse, and against his army" (Revelation 19:19). It is not recorded that they will back down or retreat. On the contrary, men under the control of Satan will actually think that they are greater than the God of heaven. Men will raise their weapons against the omnipotent God. Then Christ will speak, and the total military force of earth will be dead. The Battle of Armageddon will be over.

The aftermath of this fearful experience is recorded in the following verses:

> And I saw an angel standing in the sun; and he cried with a loud voice, saying to all the fowls that fly in the midst of heaven, Come and gather yourselves together unto the supper of the great God; that ye may eat the flesh of kings, and the flesh of captains, and the flesh of mighty men, and the flesh of horses, and of them that sit on them, and the flesh of all men, both free and bond, both small and great (Revelation 19:17-18).

The flesh-eating birds of earth will descend upon the land of Israel, where the dead armies will virtually cover the whole nation. That picture is impossible to describe as blood will flow "unto the horse bridles" (Revelation 14:20). Eagles will gather upon the carcasses (Matthew 24:28). It is called "the supper of the great God" (Revelation 19:17).

Certainly, the Battle of Armageddon will be a victory for Christ, for Satan's conquest over the world through Antichrist and the False Prophet will be over forever. The total military power of earth will be crushed. The long-awaited Kingdom Age will soon begin. Yes, the Battle of Armageddon will be a victory for God. But there will be a subtle kind of victory for Satan also. After all, his ultimate goal is to turn men from the truth, to lead them into darkness. Every soldier who dies in the Battle of Armageddon will be cast into hell. Nothing could please Satan more.

In 1968, Lehman Strauss and I had the joy of traveling throughout the Far East to conduct conferences for American missionaries, national pastors, and U.S. servicemen. Our last stop was South Vietnam. The conferences that had been scheduled among the Vietnamese were canceled because the week we arrived the destructive 122 millimeter rockets began falling on Saigon. The city was in virtual darkness, and it appeared that we had no alternative but to leave. Then the phone rang. It was Chaplain Cecil Lewis, my close friend from college days and one of the attendants in our wedding. How good it was to speak to Cecil and to hear of the tremendous opportunities he was having in Dong Ha, the last U.S. military base in South Vietnam.

Soon we were on a military plane headed for Dong Ha, located a few short miles from the demilitarized zone (DMZ) and North Vietnam. The experiences that followed will remain in our hearts forever. I shall never forget standing on a tower looking through high-powered binoculars at the war. I could see our planes as they swooped down on enemy positions, as well as returning fire from the enemy. There before my eyes was a war in progress. As I viewed that bloody conflict from a lookout tower, it occurred to me that a war was going on out on those fields that was not being reported. It was a war for the souls of men. Many of our boys died that day in that conflict near the DMZ, and even more Communists lost their lives; the sobering truth is that most of those who died went to hell. Though thousands of Christians have gone to heaven from battlefields, the majority of those who die in wars (even Americans) do not know Christ as Savior. It is possible to die for a good purpose but still spend eternity in hell! No one can claim the promise of heaven or the gift of life everlasting by putting on an American uniform. Salvation belongs only to those who have trusted the crucified, resurrected Son of God as Lord and Savior.

The greatest battle of all time will come some day. It is called the Battle of Armageddon. Every soldier will be an unbeliever. Every soldier will die. Every soldier will be cast into hades. I repeat, though the Battle of Armageddon will be a mighty victory for our Lord Jesus Christ, it will also offer a subtle kind of victory for Satan. After all, his goal is to influence people to reject Christ as Savior.

PEACE AT LAST

10

And I saw thrones, and they sat upon them, and
judgment was given unto them: and I saw the souls
of them that were beheaded for the witness of
Jesus, and for the word of God, and which had not
worshipped the beast, neither his image, neither
had received his mark upon their foreheads, or in
their hands; and they lived and reigned with Christ
a thousand years. But the rest of the dead lived not
again until the thousand years were finished. This is
the first resurrection. Blessed and holy is he that
hath part in the first resurrection: on such the second death hath no power, but they shall be priests
of God and of Christ, and shall reign with him a
thousand years (Revelation 20:4-6).

THE MILLENNIUM

After all of the bloodshed and heartache associated with the Great Tribulation, how refreshing it is
to come to this portion of God's Word. Here is the
prophecy of one thousand years of peace under Messiah's reign. Since the Latin equivalent for one thousand years is *millennium,* it has become acceptable
among students of Bible prophecy to refer to the
Kingdom Age as the millennial reign of Christ. During those days, the Lord Jesus Christ will be seated
on the throne of His father David, ruling over the affairs of men (Isaiah 9:7; Luke 1:32). At this point in
God's prophetic plan, the redeemed of all time will
be on earth to enjoy the long-awaited kingdom reign
of Christ. Those in their glorified bodies will include
saints of the Old Testament and the church age, as
well as believers who died during Tribulation days.

But there will be another group of redeemed men and women who will still be clothed in their corruptible bodies. These mortals will be those who trusted Christ as Savior during the Tribulation and did not die or were not martyred.

TRIBULATION SURVIVORS

The events of Matthew 25 enter the prophetic puzzle at this point. In that chapter, four kinds of people are introduced who will be alive following the Battle of Armageddon: wise virgins, foolish virgins, sheep, and goats.

JEWISH SURVIVORS

The "virgins" of Matthew 25:1-13 refer to Jews who are still alive following Daniel's Seventieth Week and the Battle of Armageddon. Dwight Pentecost gives six reasons for "rejecting the view that the virgins represent the church during the present age."[1] He then concurs with Schuyler English who wrote, "The ten virgins represent the remnant of Israel after the church has been taken. The five wise virgins are the believing remnant, the foolish virgins the unbelieving who only profess to be looking for Messiah's coming in power."[2] These believing and unbelieving Jews will stand before Christ in His special judgment of Tribulation survivors (Ezekiel 20:33-44). They will then be separated. The believing Jews (wise virgins) will enter the Kingdom Age still in their mortal bodies. The unbelieving Jews (foolish virgins) will be cast into hades.

Concerning this passage, John Walvoord writes,

> The annihilation of the armies that resist Christ's return will be God's judgment on the nations. After the final carnage of the Battle of Armageddon, the surviving people of the world will be judged one by one. All living Jews, the surviving nation of Israel, will be gathered from their hiding places in Palestine and throughout the world (Ezek. 39:28). Each one will face God as his judge, and none can escape this judgment. The rebels who have not accepted Christ as their Messiah prior to this second coming will be put to death (Ezek. 20:38). The rest, believing Jews who have survived the persecution of the tribulation period, will be allowed to enter the Promised Land as the first citizens of Christ's new kingdom on earth. Their hour of persecution will be finished forever, and they will receive all the blessings that have been promised to the children of Israel since the time of Abraham (see Jer. 31:31-34; Rom. 11:26, 27).[3]

GENTILE SURVIVORS

One other group of Tribulation survivors must be considered—the Gentiles. As surviving Jews will be divided into groups of believers and unbelievers, so Gentiles will be similarly divided. This separation of believing and unbelieving Gentiles is recorded in Matthew 25:31-46. Notice first the division:

> When the Son of man shall come in his glory, and all the holy angels with him, then shall he sit upon the throne of his glory: And before him shall be

> gathered all nations: and he shall separate them one
> from another, as a shepherd divideth his sheep from
> the goats: And he shall set the sheep on his right
> hand, but the goats on the left (verses 31-33).

Believing Gentiles, called "sheep," will be allowed
to join Jewish believers as they enter the kingdom.
This truth is clearly presented, beginning at verse
34:

> Then shall the King say unto them on his right
> hand, Come, ye blessed of my Father, inherit the
> kingdom prepared for you from the foundation of
> the world: For I was an hungred, and ye gave me
> meat: I was thirsty, and ye gave me drink: I was a
> stranger, and ye took me in: Naked, and ye clothed
> me: I was sick, and ye visited me: I was in prison,
> and ye came unto me. Then shall the righteous an-
> swer him, saying, Lord, when saw we thee an hun-
> gred, and fed thee? or thirsty, and gave thee drink?
> When saw we thee a stranger, and took thee in? or
> naked, and clothed thee? Or when saw we thee
> sick, or in prison, and came unto thee? And the
> King shall answer and say unto them, Verily I say
> unto you, Inasmuch as ye have done it unto one of
> the least of these my brethren, ye have done it unto
> me (verses 34-40).

There are those who lift this text out of its context. They would have us believe that the hungry,
thirsty, naked, sick, and imprisoned are people in
our day who need to be helped in their present dis-
tress. Obviously, there are millions of needy people
today who should be reached. It is not the intent of
this author to undermine Christ-honoring ministries

in jails, hospitals, orphanages, and rescue missions. Present-day believers should have a burden to reach people in every station of life in order to present the gospel story to them, but the primary interpretation of Matthew 25:35-36 has to do with conditions during the days of the Great Tribulation.

Remember, the Antichrist will be searching for all who have professed faith in Jesus Christ. Believing Jews will be fleeing for safety (Matthew 24:16-21). As they go, they will be witnessing for Jesus Christ. It will be the fulfillment of the prophecy of Matthew 24:14: "And this gospel of the kingdom shall be preached in all the world for a witness unto all nations." John records the results of this great worldwide missionary endeavor in Revelation 7:9: "After this I beheld, and, lo, a great multitude, which no man could number, of all nations, and kindreds, and people, and tongues, stood before the throne, and before the Lamb, clothed with white robes, and palms in their hands." Who are these Gentile believers? Verse 14 answers the question: "These are they which came out of great tribulation, and have washed their robes, and made them white in the blood of the Lamb." It is clear that most of those who trust Christ as Savior in Tribulation days will be martyred, but many will escape.

Now back to Matthew 25. Jesus will say to Gentile believers, "I was an hungred, and ye gave me meat: I was thirsty, and ye gave me drink: I was a stranger, and ye took me in: naked, and ye clothed me: I was sick, and ye visited me: I was in prison, and ye came unto me" (verses 35-36). Gentile believers will respond by saying, "Lord, when saw we thee an hungred, and fed thee? or thirsty, and gave thee drink? When saw we thee a stranger, and took thee in? or naked, and clothed thee?" (verses 37-38). Christ will clear the muddy waters by announcing, "Inasmuch as ye have done it unto one of the least of these my brethren, ye have done it unto me" (Matthew 25:40). When Christ speaks of His "brethren," He will be referring to His national brothers—believing Jews. As these "brethren" of Jesus Christ flee into all the world, they will be proclaiming the "gospel of the kingdom" (Matthew 24:14). Actually, their message will be the gospel of Jesus Christ. It is called the "gospel of the kingdom" because it will be preached just prior to the kingdom reign of their long-awaited Messiah. Gentiles who believe their message and trust Christ as Savior will then reach out in sympathy to their persecuted Jewish brothers. If they find a hungry Jewish believer, they will feed him. Those who are thirsty will be given drink. Strangers will be taken in. The naked will be clothed. The sick and those in prison will be visited. Please be careful not to jump to the conclusion that Gentiles will be saved because of their loving concern for Jewish believers. No one is saved because he treats Jews with respect. The only way anyone is ever born into the family of God is through simple trust in the crucified, resurrected

Lamb of Calvary; but in Tribulation days, one way to manifest that new life in Christ will be to care tenderly for Jewish brothers and sisters.

It should also be noted that unbelieving Gentiles (called goats) will manifest their rejection of Christ as Savior by their indifference and hatred toward Jewish believers.

> Then shall he say also unto them on the left hand, Depart from me, ye cursed, into everlasting fire, prepared for the devil and his angels: for I was an hungred, and ye gave me no meat: I was thirsty, and ye gave me no drink: I was a stranger, and ye took me not in: naked, and ye clothed me not: sick, and in prison, and ye visited me not. Then shall they also answer him, saying, Lord, when saw we thee an hungred, or athirst, or a stranger, or naked, or sick, or in prison, and did not minister unto thee? Then shall he answer them, saying, Verily I say unto you, Inasmuch as ye did it not to one of the least of these, ye did it not to me. And these shall go away into everlasting punishment: but the righteous into life eternal (Matthew 25:41-46).

With the exception of the Antichrist and the False Prophet, all unbelievers will be in hades at this point in the prophetic blueprint. The Antichrist and the False Prophet will be cast into the lake of fire following the Battle of Armageddon (Revelation 19:20). They will be there for one thousand years before the unbelievers in hades are cast into that horrible place. That truth will be considered in a later chapter, but the truth to be stressed now is that apart from the Antichrist and the False Prophet, all unbelievers will be in hades when Christ sets up His kingdom. It should also be noted that all of those on earth at the beginning of the Millennium will be true believers. This will be the third time in human history that earth will be totally populated with people who are in a proper relationship with God. The first time was in the Garden of Eden. There were only two people on the planet (Adam and Eve), and both of them were in fellowship with God. The second reference is to Noah and his family following the Flood. The third time that earth's total population is redeemed will be at the beginning of the millennial kingdom.

Robert Schuller, a well-known television pastor, in his book entitled *Self Esteem: The New Reformation,* states,

> When we pray, "Thy kingdom come," we are praying for the successful growth, the prospering enlargement, of the increase of the number of redeemed people, looking to the day when human beings will be inspired by kingdom persons to treat one another with respect and dignity regardless of race, religion, economic class, or politics.[4]

Though the races will maintain their identity during the Kingdom Age, it should be understood that in regard to "religion, economic class, or politics," the kingdom will be a theocracy. The Greek word *theos* means "God," so a theocracy is a God-rule.

That is exactly what the millennial kingdom will be. The Lord Jesus Christ will be seated on the throne of His father David. He alone will rule the world, so there will be no other political system. He alone will be worshiped, so there will be no man-made religions. The concept expressed by Robert Schuller that "kingdom persons [will] treat one another with respect and dignity regardless of . . . religion, economic class, or politics" is foreign to Scripture. He goes on to say, "To build self-worth in another person is the fulfillment of the prayer, 'Thy kingdom come, Thy will be done.'"[5] On the contrary, the fulfillment of this prayer will be the setting up of Christ's kingdom when His will shall be done on earth as His will is done in heaven. That condition can exist only when Christ is seated on the throne of His father David.

At the beginning of the Kingdom Age, there will be no one on earth except those who have been redeemed in the blood of God's Lamb, the Lord Jesus Christ. Joy and peace will prevail as Christ rules over the affairs of men. It will be the fulfillment of many prophecies in the Word of God. For example, Isaiah was looking forward to the theocracy when he wrote, "And he shall judge among the nations, and shall rebuke many people: and they shall beat their swords into plowshares, and their spears into pruninghooks: nation shall not lift up sword against nation, neither shall they learn war any more" (Isaiah 2:4). Isaiah also states,

> The wolf also shall dwell with the lamb, and the
> leopard shall lie down with the kid; and the calf and

the young lion and the fatling together; and a little
child shall lead them. And the cow and the bear
shall feed; their young ones shall lie down together:
and the lion shall eat straw like the ox. And the
sucking child shall play on the hole of the asp, and
the weaned child shall put his hand on the cocka-
trice' den. They shall not hurt nor destroy in all my
holy mountain: for the earth shall be full of the
knowledge of the Lord, as the waters cover the sea
(Isaiah 11:6-9).

A brief comparison between these passages with
the account of the fourth seal judgment of Revelation 6:7-8 will give the reader immediate insight
into the shocking differences between life on earth
under the reign of Christ and disaster on earth during the reign of Satan. The fourth seal judgment will
result in death for 25 percent of all the people on
this planet. Satan will use war, hunger, and ravenous
animals to accomplish his goal. Life on earth under
the reign of Christ will be a completely different
scene. There will be no war (Isaiah 2:4). For those in
their glorified bodies, there will be no hunger, for
food will not be required to sustain life. Those who
are in their mortal bodies will certainly have no food
shortage, for the implements of war will be changed
into implements for farming. "They shall beat their
swords into plowshares, and their spears into pruninghooks" (Isaiah 2:4). Ravenous animals will also
change. No doubt the very animals that Satan will
use to devour humans during Tribulation days are

seen in a tranquil state during the millennial kingdom (Isaiah 11:6-8).

My primary goal during our years as missionaries in South Vietnam was to reach the Vietnamese who lived, for the most part, on the lower elevations; but now and then I was invited to preach to the tribal people of the central highlands. After one lengthy trek to a Christian village, I was asked by the tribal pastor if I would try to kill a Bengal tiger that had been seen lurking in the area. These beautiful beasts were killing about five hundred tribal people each year, and still the South Vietnamese government would not allow tribesmen to have guns! A night of walking through the jungle with my colleague John Newman was not productive, so we decided that we would kill a bait and stake it at the base of a large tree several miles from the village. A few days later the pastor told me that the bait was "ripe." Believe me, it was "ripe"! I climbed the tree and sat on a small platform about twenty feet over the dead bait. That night the tiger came. I shall never forget the sound of his licking the bait. I could not see him on the dark jungle floor, but I knew he was a big one—certainly, the king of the Vietnamese jungle. Needless to say, the thought never entered my mind to come down out of the tree, pat him gently on the head, climb on his back, and take a ride through the jungle. I never entertained that thought because we are not living in the Millennium; but during the days of Christ's earthly reign, even the animal kingdom will be at peace, and the redeemed will be able to enjoy creatures that were once off-limits. My son, Dan, who was born in Vietnam, and I are planning to visit those jungles during millennial days. We have already made plans to find a couple of tigers and enjoy a ride through those beautiful mountains. You are invited to join us if you like. Of course, you must know Christ as Savior, for only those who have been born into the family of God will be allowed to enter those days of peace.

THE FINAL REVOLT

It would be refreshing if God's prophetic blueprint revealed no further heartache or death, but such is not the case. The record of things to come includes Revelation 20:7-9:

> And when the thousand years are expired, Satan shall be loosed out of his prison, and shall go out to deceive the nations which are in the four quarters of the earth, Gog and Magog, to gather them together to battle: the number of whom is as the sand of the sea. And they went up on the breadth of the earth, and compassed the camp of the saints about, and the beloved city: and fire came down from God out of heaven, and devoured them.

In the chapter that follows, the subject of Satan and his future will be dealt with; but for our present consideration, please notice that the millennial reign of Christ will end with revolt: "Satan shall be loosed out of his prison, and shall go out to deceive the nations . . . to gather them together to battle" (Revelation 20:7-8). This will be Satan's final "fling," his last opportunity to influence mortals to rebel against the authority of Almighty God. The question that immediately rises is "Where do these rebels come from?" It was noted earlier that every person on earth will be saved when the kingdom begins, but as the kingdom ends, there will be so many unbelievers that they will number "as the sand of the sea" (Revelation 20:8).

As has already been stated, Scripture records three times when every person on earth was a true believer: Adam and Eve in the Garden of Eden; Noah and his family following the Flood; and the entire family of redeemed saints at the beginning of the millennial kingdom. It should be noted that Adam's children were sinners, Noah's descendants turned from God, and someday children born in the kingdom will be totally depraved and, like all of Adam's children, will need to come to Christ for salvation. These will be children of mortals who survived the awful days of the Great Tribulation. Saints in their incorruptible bodies will not be producing children. In that respect they will be like the angels of heaven (Mark 12:25).

As the Millennium progresses, mortal men will continue to reproduce after their own kind until, at the end of the kingdom reign, the earth will be repopulated with sinful men. Since Christ will be ruling (Revelation 20:4-6), and Satan will be chained in the bottomless pit (Revelation 20:1-3), there will be no outbreak of open rebellion against the authority of Christ. But Adam's nature will be very much alive deep in the hearts of those who are born in millennial days. They who refuse to trust Christ as Savior will be the ones who make up the great army that Satan will assemble as he is loosed from his prison and is allowed to return to earth for his last act of open rebellion against God. The results are found in the following verses:

> And they went up on the breadth of the earth, and compassed the camp of the saints about, and the beloved city: and fire came down from God out of heaven, and devoured them. And the devil that deceived them was cast into the lake of fire and brimstone, where the beast and the false prophet are, and shall be tormented day and night for ever and ever (Revelation 20:9-10).

More will be said concerning Satan and those who submit to him in the chapter that follows.

THE SERPENT CRAWLS
THROUGH BIBLE
PROPHECY

11

From the dawn of creation until this present hour, Satan's influence among men has been profound. But according to Bible prophecy, his power will be felt in an even greater way in the days ahead. The subject at hand deals primarily with things to come; but before considering God's prophetic blueprint as it relates to Satan, it would be good to take a brief look into history, as well as a glimpse of the present.

SATAN IN HISTORY

First, we will look at Satan's past.

> How art thou fallen from heaven, O Lucifer, son of the morning! how art thou cut down to the ground, which didst weaken the nations! For thou hast said in thine heart, I will ascend into heaven, I will exalt my throne above the stars of God: I will sit also upon the mount of the congregation, in the sides of the north: I will ascend above the heights of the clouds; I will be like the most High. Yet thou shalt be brought down to hell, to the sides of the pit. They that see thee shall narrowly look upon thee, and consider thee, saying, Is this the man that made the earth to tremble, that did shake kingdoms; That made the world as a wilderness, and destroyed the cities thereof; that opened not the house of his prisoners? (Isaiah 14:12-17).

This passage records the account of Lucifer's fall and the prophecy concerning his eternal destiny. Much has happened, and will yet take place, before the prophecy is fulfilled. But where is Satan in this present age?

SATAN TODAY

Note first that Satan has access into the presence of God. Job 2:1 declares, "Again there was a day when the sons of God came to present themselves before the Lord, and Satan came also among them to present himself before the Lord." The question arises, "Why is Satan allowed to appear before Almighty God?" The answer is recorded in Revelation 12:10, where Satan is pictured standing before God as the "accuser of our brethren." Every Christian should be careful to maintain a consistent testimony because God is not the only one who is viewing our lives. Satan is also aware of our deportment and is quick to make accusations before the throne of God.

Next, we understand that Satan has access to the earth. Job 2:2 goes on to state, "And the Lord said unto Satan, From whence comest thou? And Satan answered the Lord, and said, From going to and fro in the earth, and from walking up and down in it." Sometime ago, I heard of a liberal pastor who wrote, "There is no such thing as a devil." A certain Christian read that statement and responded by saying, "I feel like the prizefighter who was receiving a terrible beating at the hands of his opponent. As the weary boxer leaned on the ropes about to fall, his manager said, 'Come on, he is not even hitting you.' The fighter replied, 'He isn't? Then watch that referee because somebody is!'" The inference is clear. If there is no Devil, who is responsible for the things that only Satan can do? Alfred Hough had this in mind when he penned this satire:

> Men don't believe in the Devil now, as their fathers
> used to do.
> They've forced the door of the broadest creed to
> let his majesty through.
> There isn't a print of his cloven foot or fiery dart
> from his bow
> To be found on earth or air today, for the world has
> voted it so.
> Who dogs the steps of the toiling saint and digs the
> pits for his feet?
> Who sows the tares in the fields of time whenever
> God sows the wheat?
> The Devil is voted not to be, and of course, the
> thing is true,
> But who is doing the kind of work that the Devil
> alone can do?
> We are told that he doesn't go about as a roaring
> lion now,
> But whom shall we hold responsible for the ever-
> lasting row
> To be heard in home, in church and state, to the
> earth's remotest bound,
> If the Devil by unanimous vote is nowhere to be
> found?
> Won't someone step to the front forthwith and
> make his bow and show
> How the frauds and crimes of a single day spring
> up? We want to know.
> The Devil was fairly voted out, and of course, the
> Devil's gone;
> But simple people would like to know, who carries
> the business on?

God's Word is clear on this subject. "Be sober, be vigilant; because your adversary the devil, as a roaring lion, walketh about, seeking whom he may devour" (I Peter 5:8).

Satan not only has access into the presence of God, where he accuses the brethren night and day, and access upon the earth where he roams as a roaring lion; but he is also showing his presence in outer space. The apostle Paul declares, "Put on the whole armour of God, that ye may be able to stand against the wiles of the devil. For we wrestle not against flesh and blood, but against principalities, against powers, against the rulers of the darkness of this world, against spiritual wickedness in high places" (Ephesians 6:11-12). Earlier in this epistle Paul refers to Satan as "the prince of the power of the air" (Ephesians 2:2).

It is interesting to note the enchantment that people seem to have with life in outer space. From many modern-day psychics and astrologers, statements about UFOs have become commonplace: "Some day soon UFOs will be landing upon the earth." "Representatives from other planets are gathering for an interplanetary meeting." "Contact with earth by a civilization in outer space." Many people claim to have seen UFOs. Even scientists, astronauts, and pilots are numbered with this group. "NASA delighted the media when it announced on August 7, 1996, that a meteorite from Mars shows evidence of extraterrestrial life."[1] NASA's missions to Mars, with the

Pathfinder and the Mars Surveyor Lander to study the surface of Mars, and Voyager 1 and 2, sent to study the outer planets, have renewed interest in the possibility of life beyond earth. The popularity of Hollywood ventures such as *Star Trek* and *The X-Files* is further evidence of interest in UFOs and extraterrestrial life.

It seems clear that Satan is not only getting the world ready for the coming of Antichrist, but is also, no doubt, preparing men for the Rapture of the church. Though Scripture does not record what will appear in newspapers following the catching away of the bride of Christ, it may be reported that UFOs have finally arrived and have successfully snatched away millions of people who called themselves Christians. It should not startle believers to hear of all of the strange events associated with outer space, for remember that this is Satan's domain.

SATAN IN PROPHECY

The day is coming, however, when Satan will be cast out of the atmospheric and celestial heavens above us. This truth is presented clearly in Revelation 12:7-12:

> And there was war in heaven: Michael and his angels fought against the dragon; and the dragon fought and his angels, And prevailed not; neither was their place found any more in heaven. And the

great dragon was cast out, that old serpent, called
the Devil, and Satan, which deceiveth the whole
world: he was cast out into the earth, and his angels
were cast out with him. And I heard a loud voice
saying in heaven, Now is come salvation, and
strength, and the kingdom of our God, and the
power of his Christ: for the accuser of our brethren
is cast down, which accused them before our God
day and night. And they overcame him by the blood
of the Lamb, and by the word of their testimony;
and they loved not their lives unto the death.
Therefore rejoice, ye heavens, and ye that dwell in
them. Woe to the inhabiters of the earth and of the
sea! for the devil is come down unto you, having
great wrath, because he knoweth that he hath but a
short time.

Lucifer lost his first estate, as was noted earlier in
Isaiah 14. Now in Revelation 12, a fearful battle is
waged between the forces of heaven and the forces
of Satan (Lucifer). Michael and the angels of heaven
will win the war, so those in heaven can rejoice over
God's great victory. But "woe to the inhabiters of the
earth and of the sea! for the devil is come down unto
you, having great wrath, because he knoweth that he
hath but a short time" (Revelation 12:12). As the
chart on page ix suggests, this battle will take place
in the middle of the Seventieth Week of Daniel.

At that point, Satan will be cast to the earth, no
longer permitted to appear in the presence of God
or to roam in the celestial heavens above. He will be
confined to the earth. It is interesting to note that
Revelation 12:7-12 records the casting out of Satan

to the earth, and in the following verses, the Great Tribulation is introduced. During the three and one-half years that follow, Satan will do all within his power to kill as many people on earth as possible. His special hatred will be aimed at those who trust Christ as Savior, but he will also feel a fiendish glee over the millions of unbelievers who die without Christ and without hope. Jesus declared in Matthew 24:22, "And except those days should be shortened, there should no flesh be saved." It would appear that if Satan had but a few more months, his goal of ridding the earth of its total population would be accomplished. It should be understood that many of the judgments that will take place in those days will be from the hand of God against a wicked and perverse generation, but it will be Satan who will put into the hearts of nations the desire for battle. He will also bring untold misery through hunger and ravenous animals. It will certainly be the most chaotic time in human history. It has been properly called "the Great Tribulation."

THE BOTTOMLESS PIT

As the serpent continues to crawl through the prophetic scene, the next major development will be his confinement in the bottomless pit.

> And I saw an angel come down from heaven, having the key of the bottomless pit and a great chain in his hand. And he laid hold on the dragon, that old serpent, which is the Devil, and Satan, and bound

him a thousand years, and cast him into the bottomless pit, and shut him up, and set a seal upon
him, that he should deceive the nations no more,
till the thousand years should be fulfilled: and after
that he must be loosed a little season (Revelation
20:1-3).

This confinement will follow the Battle of Armageddon. The thousand years that Satan will be
chained will be the same thousand years in which
Christ will be ruling in His kingdom. The prayer
that has been offered for nearly two thousand years
will at last be answered. "Our Father which art in
heaven, Hallowed be thy name. Thy kingdom come.
Thy will be done in earth, as it is in heaven"
(Matthew 6:9-10). The will of God may be done
today in the hearts of those who have trusted Christ
as Savior, but God's will will never be done on earth
as His will is done in heaven until Satan is chained in
the bottomless pit and Christ is sitting upon the
throne of His father David.

SATAN LOOSED

One would think that after a thousand-year
prison term Satan would learn something; but the
sacred record tells us that after a millennium in the
bottomless pit, Satan will be loosed out of his prison
and will go out to deceive the nations. He will
gather all of those who have been born in the Millennium and have failed to trust Christ as Savior into
one last rebellious army. They will follow Satan's

leadership in defying the exalted position of Jesus Christ, but they will meet the wrath of God. More will be said on this subject in the chapter that follows, but for our present consideration, Revelation 20:10 becomes a fitting conclusion: "And the devil that deceived them was cast into the lake of fire and brimstone, where the beast and the false prophet are, and shall be tormented day and night for ever and ever." It should be understood that Satan will be cast into the lake of fire where the Beast and the False Prophet are. The word is *are,* not *were.* That is, at this point, the Antichrist and the False Prophet will have been in the lake of fire for a thousand years. It should be remembered that they will be cast into the lake of fire following the Battle of Armageddon (Revelation 19:20).

Satan will finally be cast into the same place a thousand years later only to discover the Antichrist and the False Prophet are still there. Those who argue that the lake of fire is a place of annihilation certainly have a difficult time explaining Revelation 20:10. We can rejoice that Satan will be in the lake of fire for all eternity. After all, that place was "prepared for the devil and his angels" (Matthew 25:41). It was never God's intention that any human being should go to hell, but those who reject His Son as Savior will be cast into that eternal place (Revelation 20:15). As sure as God's Word is true, they will spend the countless ages to come with Satan.

Earlier in this chapter, a passage from Isaiah 14 was presented. I would like to close this chapter with that same portion of God's revelation. "Yet thou shalt be brought down to hell, to the sides of the pit. They that see thee shall narrowly look upon thee, and consider thee, saying, Is this the man that made the earth to tremble, that did shake kingdoms; That made the world as a wilderness" (Isaiah 14:15-17a). What a tragedy to think that some who read these words may actually repeat this passage in Satan's ears as they suffer the torments of hell throughout all eternity.

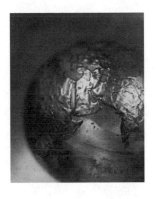

UNBELIEVERS IN PROPHECY

12

God's Word is clear concerning the destiny of those who die without Christ. In brief, it can be stated that there are four steps awaiting the unsaved: hades (Luke 16:19-24), "the resurrection of damnation" (John 5:29), the Great White Throne Judgment (Revelation 20:11-13), and the lake of fire (Revelation 20:15).

TWO KINDS OF UNBELIEVERS

The question to be considered in this chapter deals with the prophecy concerning unbelievers here on earth. It should be understood that immediately after the Rapture of the church, every person on earth will be an unbeliever; but it should also be noted that there will be two kinds of unbelievers: those who have heard the gospel and have rejected God's plan of redemption, and those who have never heard. Concerning those who will have heard but said no to Jesus Christ, Paul wrote, "because they received not the love of the truth, that they might be saved. And for this cause God shall send them strong delusion, that they should believe a lie: That they all might be damned who believed not the truth, but had pleasure in unrighteousness" (II Thessalonians 2:10b-12). There is considerable discussion concerning this passage. Some are strong in their belief that those who hear the gospel before the Rapture may still be saved after the Rapture. It is the conviction of this author that those who "received not the love of the truth, that they might be saved" is a reference to people living before the Rapture who heard the story of God's love and could have been saved, but they turned from God's grace. These will be the ones who shall be sent a "strong delusion, that they should believe a lie." In other words, they would not believe the truth, who is Jesus Christ, so they will believe the lie, who is the Antichrist. The record goes on to say "that they all might be damned who believed not the truth."

The late H. A. Ironside had this to say on the passage before us:

> I have run across the error in many recent books on the coming of the Lord. That after the rapture of the church there will be a great revival, an unprecedented spiritual awakening in Christendom, when a vast number of people who have been undecided during the present dispensation of grace will turn to the Lord; and it is being widely taught that these will form the great multitude of Gentiles who will be saved out of the tribulation. Let me say, I have searched my Bible diligently for any confirmation of such teaching, but I fail to find it. On the contrary, we are distinctly told in II Thessalonians 2:11 that God is going to give up those who during this present age receive not the love of the truth that they might be saved; they will be given up to hardness of heart and perversity of spirit.[1]

There will be another group of unsaved people on earth following the Rapture of the church, namely, people who have never had an intelligent opportunity to accept or reject the Lord Jesus Christ as personal Savior. They will, no doubt, come from every nation on earth, for in the revelation given to God's servant John, he sees a great host of believers coming out of the Great Tribulation. These believers will come from "all nations, and kindreds, and people, and tongues" (Revelation 7:9). The 144,000 Jews who will be saved, 12,000 from each of the twelve tribes of Israel, are simply the "firstfruits unto God and to the Lamb" (Revelation 14:4); but by no means will they be the only fruit. Following their conversion will be the salvation of millions of other Jews, as well as the host of Gentiles mentioned above, a multitude so numerous that "no man could number [them]" (Revelation 7:9).

This chapter, however, is primarily concerned with unbelievers as they appear in the prophetic blueprint here on earth. The next scene to be considered is in Matthew 24:37-42, where the following is recorded:

> But as the days of Noe were, so shall also the coming of the Son of man be. For as in the days that were before the flood they were eating and drinking, marrying and giving in marriage, until the day that Noe entered into the ark, and knew not until the flood came, and took them all away; so shall also the coming of the Son of man be. Then shall two be in the field; the one shall be taken, and the other left. Two women shall be grinding at the mill; the one shall be taken, and the other left. Watch therefore: for ye know not what hour your Lord doth come.

It was suggested earlier that the Rapture of the church is not found in the Synoptic Gospels (Matthew, Mark, and Luke), but many people use the passage just quoted as a text for Christ's coming for His bride. The fact is, the reference to "the coming of the Son of man" (Matthew 24:37) is not a reference to Christ's coming for His bride but to His coming to the earth in His Revelation. In this coming of Christ, He will destroy the armies of earth in the Battle of Armageddon (Matthew 24:27-28). It will take place after the Great Tribulation (Matthew 24:29). Every eye will see Him as He returns in His power and great glory (Matthew 24:30-31; Acts 1:11). There are those who reason that since "two [shall] be in the field; the one shall be taken, and the other left" (Matthew 24:40), the passage must be speaking of the Rapture of the church. After all, if a believer and an unbeliever are in a field together when the church is raptured, the believer will be caught away and the unbeliever will be left. However, Matthew 24 is not dealing with the Rapture of the church but with the Revelation of Christ. Then what can be said about those who will be taken and those who will be left? Remember, Jesus precedes this announcement with the prophecy that there will be a repeat performance of the days of Noah. That wicked generation refused to believe the truth, and finally "the flood came, and took them all away" (Matthew 24:39). It is clear from this text, as well as from the Old Testament account, that all of those who were taken away were unbelievers. Those who were left were believers who became the first of a new generation on earth. So it will be when Christ returns to the earth in His Revelation. The survivors of earth will be gathered to be judged by Jesus Christ. The unbelievers who have come through the Great Tribulation and failed to trust Christ as Savior will be cast into hades, as were the unbelievers of Noah's day. The Jewish unbelievers are called "foolish" virgins, while the Gentile unbelievers are referred to as "goats" (Matthew 25). Jewish believers are called "wise" virgins, while Gentile believers are referred to as "sheep." These believers, like Noah and his family, will become the progenitors of a new race that will develop here on earth during Christ's millennial reign.

John Walvoord has written the following on the subject:

> A utopian world will follow the colossal failure of man's attempt to control human history. Three judgments will have purged the world of all who have not believed in Jesus Christ. The armies of the world will have been destroyed on the battlefields of the Middle East. Unbelieving Jews will have been judged and killed. In the judgment of the sheep and goats, unbelieving non-Jews will also have been purged from the earth. The entire adult population of the earth which remains will have experienced regeneration through faith in Christ.[2]

THE GREAT WHITE THRONE

There is one final step that must be included in a study of unbelievers in Bible prophecy—the Great White Throne Judgment.

> And I saw a great white throne, and him that sat on it, from whose face the earth and the heaven fled away; and there was found no place for them. And I saw the dead, small and great, stand before God; and the books were opened: and another book was opened, which is the book of life: and the dead were judged out of those things which were written in the books, according to their works (Revelation 20:11-12).

All of the unsaved in the history of man will stand before Jesus Christ at this judgment (John 5:22; Acts 17:31; II Peter 2:9). At that awesome judgment, the books will be opened. These books contain the evil works of all of those who stand before Christ, for they will be "judged out of those things which were written in the books, according to their works" (Revelation 20:12). What a sobering truth to realize that God has been keeping accurate records of the thoughts, words, and actions of all of those who have ever violated His standards.

It is also recorded that the "book of life" will be opened. I agree with the comment in the footnote of the Scofield Bible: "The book of life is there to answer such as plead their works for justification . . . an awful blank where the name might have been." In Jeremiah 2:8 we read of those who handled the law of God but did not know Him, and in Jeremiah 23:21 God declared, "I have not sent these prophets, yet they ran: I have not spoken to them, yet they prophesied." Being a part of the modern-day clergy does not insure a person of eternal life, for Jesus declared: "Many will say to me in that day, Lord, Lord, have we not prophesied in thy name? and in thy name have cast out devils? and in thy name done many wonderful works? And then will I profess unto them, I never knew you: depart from me, ye that work iniquity" (Matthew 7:22-23). The fact is that no number of works, however good they might be, can insure a person of life eternal. "For by grace are ye saved through faith; and that not of yourselves: it is the gift of God: Not of works, lest any man should boast" (Ephesians 2:8-9).

The only work that insures life eternal is the finished work of Christ upon the cross. Whoever will come to Him in childlike faith may pass from death unto life. If you have never opened your life to God's crucified, resurrected Lamb, I urge you at this moment to call upon Him as a penitent sinner, admitting your need and inviting Him to come into your heart as Lord and Savior.

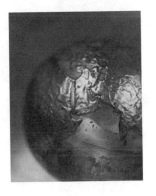

QUESTIONS AND ANSWERS 13

It has been my observation in recent years that Christians have become increasingly interested in Bible prophecy. That interest is bringing about a healthy desire to sound the depths of prophetic truth revealed in God's precious Word. In churches where I have gone to conduct prophecy conferences, believers have asked many questions on this vital subject. I hope most of them have been answered in the preceding chapters. It is my desire to conclude this book by addressing those questions that have not been dealt with thus far.

Question: Why will the church be raptured prior to the Seventieth Week of Daniel?

Answer: In Daniel 9:24 we read, "Seventy weeks are determined upon thy people and upon thy holy city." It is clear that this prophecy was to affect the nation of Israel. The people of Daniel were the Jews. Since the church was not found in the first sixty-nine weeks that have already come and gone, there is no reason to place it in the Seventieth Week that is yet to appear. It should also be noted that the Seventieth Week does not begin with the Rapture of the church but with the signing of the covenant between the Antichrist and the nation of Israel (Daniel 9:27). Since he will not be revealed until after the church is raptured (II Thessalonians 2:7-8), it is logical to deduce that the church cannot be on earth during the Seventieth Week. In addition, it is an interesting fact that after the church is spoken of in Revelation 3, it is not referred to as being on earth until after the Battle

of Armageddon in Revelation 19. The bride of
Christ is pictured in heaven during Tribulation days
(Revelation 19:7-10).

Question: What are the differences between the
Judgment Seat of Christ and the Great White
Throne Judgment?

Answer: In the preceding chapter we considered
the Great White Throne Judgment, which takes place
following the millennial kingdom. It will be a judgment of works for all unbelievers and will determine
degrees of punishment that will be their portion in the
lake of fire throughout eternity (Revelation 20:11-15).
No believer will stand before Jesus at the Great
White Throne Judgment.

The Judgment Seat of Christ will follow the Rapture of the church and will take place at least 1,007
years before the Great White Throne Judgment. It
will also be a judgment of works (II Corinthians
5:10) to determine degrees of reward for believers
who will enjoy eternity with Jesus Christ. No fewer
than five crowns will be given to saints of God who
have labored faithfully for Him:

1. The incorruptible crown (I Corinthians 9:25)
2. The crown of life (James 1:12; Revelation
   2:10)
3. The crown of glory (I Peter 5:4)
4. The crown of rejoicing (I Thessalonians 2:19)
5. The crown of righteousness (II Timothy 4:8)

Question: How can the Rapture be imminent when
the gospel has not yet been preached in all tongues?

Answer: This question has its roots in Matthew 24:14, where we read, "And this gospel of the kingdom shall be preached in all the world for a witness unto all nations; and then shall the end come." It should be understood that the "gospel of the kingdom" is the same as the gospel we preach today as far as its content is concerned. It is called the "gospel of the kingdom" in Matthew 24 because it will be preached just prior to the Kingdom Age. Jesus is speaking here of the great missionary outreach that will take place during Tribulation days following the Rapture of the church. In the revelation, John sees the extent of that worldwide spiritual awakening: "After this I beheld, and, lo, a great multitude, which no man could number, of all nations, and kindreds, and people, and tongues, stood before the throne, and before the Lamb, clothed with white robes, and palms in their hands" (Revelation 7:9). In other words, Matthew 24:14 is not talking about world evangelism that must take place before the Rapture. The church is not commissioned to go into all the world to preach the gospel to every creature so that Christ may return to rapture His bride. Our obedience must be based on the clear command and compassion of Jesus (Mark 16:15; II Peter 3:9).

Question: Will Christians know who the Antichrist is before the Rapture?

Answer: It is the conviction of some noted students of Bible prophecy that the Antichrist will be Judas Iscariot restored to life. Those who believe that

Satan does not have the power to bring one back to life are more comfortable with the position that the Antichrist will be another man who will be filled and controlled by Satan as Judas was. If this position is true, then it is possible that we could be seeing the Antichrist today but not know it is he. For that matter, if he is alive at this hour, he is not aware of the part he will someday play in Bible prophecy. Whichever position you take (I prefer the latter), the fact remains that believers will be removed from this earthly scene before the wicked one is revealed (II Thessalonians 2:7-8).

Question: When will the Antichrist seize total power over all the earth?

Answer: According to Daniel 7:8, Antichrist will seize immediate control of three of the ten nations in the revived Roman Empire. Shortly thereafter, he will gain control over the seven remaining nations. With the destruction of the great northern confederacy headed up by Russia (Ezekiel 38), Antichrist will then become the undisputed ruler of the world (Revelation 13:7).

Question: Who are the 144,000?

Answer: In Revelation 7 we are introduced to a special group of believers who are called "the servants of our God" (Revelation 7:3). They are later referred to as "the firstfruits unto God and to the Lamb" (Revelation 14:4). These will be the first to come to Christ as Savior following the Rapture of the church, and they will number 144,000. In Revelation 7 we read that they will come out of the tribes of Israel, 12,000 from each of the 12 tribes. One note of clarification should be made: The tribe of Dan is excluded (Revelation 7:6), and Manasseh (one of the sons of Joseph) takes his place. We are not told why this change is made, but some have suggested that it is because the tribe of Dan was always one of the first to go into idolatry (Judges 18:30). Jacob's prophecy concerning his son Dan may also be a factor (Genesis 49:17).

Question: Will any believers be in the Battle of Armageddon?

Answer: When Christ returns in His revelation to destroy the total military power of earth and to bring to an end Satan's reign of terror, the Tribulation saints who are still alive will be either in prison or in hiding. Since they will have refused the mark of the beast, they will not be a part of the political, social, or economic community of Antichrist.

Question: Will there be death during the millennial reign of Christ?

Answer: It was observed in an earlier chapter that all of those who are with Christ at the dawn of the Millennium will be true believers. All will have glorified bodies with the exception of those who lived through the Great Tribulation. Those mortals will become the progenitors of a new race on earth. Those born in millennial days must receive Christ as Savior just as people in prior dispensations. It is unthinkable, but true, that millions of people born under the perfect conditions of Christ's kingdom will still refuse to accept Him as Savior. From Isaiah's prophecy, it is learned that "There shall be no more thence an infant of days, nor an old man that hath not filled his days: for the child shall die an hundred years old; but the sinner being an hundred years old shall be accursed" (Isaiah 65:20). Apparently, in the theocracy, even with Satan in the bottomless pit, some unbelievers will exert their Adamic nature to the point that they must be judged on an individual basis and cast into hades. Since longevity will be restored during millennial days, it will seem that a hundred-year-old person who dies is like a child. All unbelievers will come together when Satan is released from the bottomless pit (Revelation 20:7) in a mighty display of rebellion against the rule of Jesus Christ. The fire of God will then fall from heaven and devour that great host (Revelation 20:8-9). They will be the last mortals to taste of physical death.

Question: What will follow the Great White Throne Judgment?

Answer: The final judgment of God will be upon the earth and the heavens. The apostle Peter wrote, "Looking for and hasting unto the coming of the day of God, wherein the heavens being on fire shall be dissolved, and the elements shall melt with fervent heat? Nevertheless we, according to his promise, look for new heavens and a new earth, wherein dwelleth righteousness" (II Peter 3:12-13). The timing of this final judgment is found in Revelation 21:1, where, following the Great White Throne Judgment, John declares, "And I saw a new heaven and a new earth: for the first heaven and the first earth were passed away; and there was no more sea." Those who have trusted God's Son as Savior will enjoy His fellowship under perfect conditions throughout eternity.

Question: Please explain the seventy-five-day period between the Seventieth Week and the Millennium.

Answer: Please read Daniel 12:11-12. The day is coming when Antichrist will sign a covenant with Israel (Daniel 9:27). The signing of this peace treaty will officially start a seven-year period of time we call the Seventieth Week of Daniel. It is a period of 2,520 days (see chart, page viii). But "in the midst of the week [that is, after 1,260 days] he shall cause the sacrifice and the oblation to cease" (Daniel 9:27). At that time he will place an image, like himself, in the temple. Jesus called this "the abomination of desolation" (Matthew 24:15).

Since this will happen at the halfway point of the Seventieth Week, we conclude there will be exactly 1,260 days until the end of the Seventieth Week. However, Daniel 12:11 tells us that the duration of the abomination will continue for 1,290 days. This represents a thirty-day extension. Daniel 12:12 goes on to say, "Blessed is he that waiteth, and cometh to the thousand three hundred and five and thirty days." That is, the total period of time from the middle of the week (when the "sacrifice shall be taken away") until the end of this piece of the prophetic puzzle will be 1335 days, and 1335 days minus 1260 days equals 75 days. In other words, verse 11 tells us of a thirty-day extension. An added 45 days are found in verse 12. During these 75 days the following will take place: The Revelation of Christ will occur (Revelation 19:11-19), the Antichrist and the False Prophet will be cast into the lake of fire (Revelation 19:20), Satan will be cast into the bottomless pit (Revelation 20:1-3), and the survivors of the Great Tribulation will be judged (Matthew 25:1-13, 31-46).

Question: If the first 69 weeks (483 years) of Daniel's vision (Daniel 9:24-26*a*) began March 14, 445 B.C., and ended April 6, A.D. 32 (on the Julian calendar), is there not a discrepancy of dates between the Jewish and Julian calendars?

Answer: It must be remembered that the Jewish calendar has 360 days in a year. The Julian (now Gregorian) calendar has 365 days. If one calculates the time of the end of the sixty-ninth week on the Jewish calendar, one must multiply

$$\begin{array}{r} 483 \text{ years} \\ \times \quad 360 \text{ days} \\ \hline 173{,}880 \text{ days} \end{array}$$

Both Sir Robert Anderson and Dr. Alva J. McClain have analyzed this same period on the Julian calendar. Here are their findings: March 14, 445 B.C., to April 6, A.D. 32, requires 476 years (1 B.C. to A.D. 1 is one year). (See *The Coming Prince* by Sir Robert

Anderson and *Daniel's Prophecy of the Seventy Weeks* by Dr. Alva J. McClain.)

$$\begin{array}{r}
476 \text{ years} \\
\times \quad 365 \text{ days} \\
\hline
173,740 \text{ days} \\
116 \text{ days} \\
+ \quad 24 \text{ days} \\
\hline
173,880 \text{ days}
\end{array}$$

476 years

× 365 days

173,740 days

116 days (add for leap years)

+ 24 days (add for March 14 to April 6 inclusive)

173,880 days

Daniel's 69 weeks on the Jewish and the Julian calendars are the same, 173,880 days. The sixty-ninth week ended on Sunday, Palm Sunday, before the Crucifixion. The prophecy of Daniel states that after 69 weeks "shall Messiah be cut off." That is, Jesus will be crucified. History now records that 173,880 days passed from the time Artaxerxes gave the command to Nehemiah to restore and build Jerusalem until the day that Christ rode into that city on a colt (see chart, page vii). Later that week, as Daniel foretold, Jesus suffered, bled, and died for the sin of the world. The price of our redemption was fully paid. The pivotal point of God's revelation to man was seen by Daniel—"Messiah [was] cut off."

Now may I offer one final observation as I conclude this book on Bible prophecy. No one has eternal life because he believes what God will accomplish in the future. We are not saved by what God will do, but by what God has done. If you want life everlasting, you must look back to Calvary. It was there that

Jesus took upon Himself the sin of the world, shed His blood, and gave His life. If you have never trusted this crucified, resurrected Lamb of God as your Savior, I urge you to come to Him now. Pray a prayer like this:

> Oh, God, I confess that I am a sinner and repent of my sin. I believe You love me, in spite of my sin, and sent Your Son to earth to bear my sin in His body on the cross. Lord Jesus, I believe You shed Your blood and gave Your life as the only atonement for my sin. I also believe You arose from the dead. I ask You to enter my life. Be merciful to me, a sinner, and save me now.

NOTES

Chapter 1

1. J. Wilbur Chapman, "One Day."

Chapter 2

1. H. A. Ironside, *Daniel* (Neptune, N.J.: Loizeaux Brothers, 1911), p. 137.

Chapter 3

1. *Webster's New Biographical Dictionary,* s.v. "Artaxerxes."

2. Robert Anderson, *The Coming Prince* (Grand Rapids, Mich.: Kregel Publications, 1963), p. 123.

3. Ibid., pp. 127-28.

Chapter 4

1. "A Conversation with Ronald Steel: 'We Are in a Time of Pygmies When It Comes to Leaders,'" *U.S. News and World Report* 89, no. 15 (1980): 58.

Chapter 5

1. Jack Egan, "Banks: Now You See 'Em, Soon You May Not," *U.S. News and World Report* 127, no. 14 (1999): 54.

2. "Cash Technologies Eyes Your ATM Card," *Business Week,* no. 3659 (1999): 209.

Chapter 6

1. J. Dwight Pentecost, *Things to Come* (Grand Rapids, Mich.: Zondervan, 1958), p. 331.

2. Henry Kissinger, Excerpt from *"The White House Years," Time* 114, no. 15 (1979): 43.

3. Mindy Belz and Beverly Nickles, "War Without End, Alas," *World* 14, no. 50 (1999): 25.

4. Murray Gart and Abu Said Abu Rish, "An Interview with Arafat," *Time* 114, no. 8 (1979): 27.

5. William Griffith, "The Real Stakes in Afghanistan," *Reader's Digest* 116, no. 698 (1980): 48.

6. *Decision* 1, no. 8 (1961): n.p.

Chapter 9

1. John F. Walvoord with John E. Walvoord, *Armageddon* (Grand Rapids, Mich.: Zondervan, 1974), pp. 164-65.

Chapter 10

1. Pentecost, *Things to Come,* p. 283.

2. Schuyler English, *Studies in the Gospel According to Matthew*, p. 173, quoted in Pentecost, *Things to Come,* p. 283.

3. John F. Walvoord with John E. Walvoord, *Armageddon,* pp. 177-78.

4. Robert Schuller, *Self Esteem: The New Reformation* (Waco, Tex.: Word Books, 1982), p. 72.

5. Ibid., p. 76.

Chapter 11

1. "Life on Mars?" *Teacher's Resource Guide to Current Events* 1998-99, (Greenville, S.C.: BJU Press, 1998), p. 194

Chapter 12

1. H. A. Ironside, *Lectures on the Revelation* (Neptune, N.J.: Loizeaux Brothers, 1920), pp. 133-34.

2. John F. Walvoord with John E. Walvoord, *Armageddon,* p. 179.